Introduction

It started with a very simple i
Yorkshire. My step daughter lives
time I visit one of these towns i am struck by the contrast.
They share a name but appear to have little else in common.

Whenever I have walked around Bradford in Avon everything about the town has seemed to give off an air of comfortable pleasurable success. People look well dressed and healthy and the shops seem full of nice things to buy. A gentle river rolls through the outskirts of the town past well kept parks and houses built out of a beautiful golden stone can be seen climbing the steep slopes of the hillside above it. By comparison Bradford seems to reek of neglect and decline. People in the streets don't look remotely well off. There are pound shops and pawn brokers in the city centre streets. There is something of a river but it isn't a thing of beauty. It isn't even graced by being granted the name. Bradford Beck is hidden away. At first behind tatty disused warehouses, then on the wrong side of some neglected sports fields before finally it is enclosed underground as if it is something the city should be ashamed of. Along with so much else of its reputation. Including riots and a set of deprivation statistics that can compete with almost anywhere in the country.

Yet I know that this image of Bradford isn't quite right. I worked there for three years and have lived close to it for twenty and so I have had the chance to find out that there is a lot more to the city than a hard working place where money had once been made and then sucked out and taken away by folks who wanted to spend it somewhere more genteel. Bradford Yorkshire has some fascinating and vibrant sides to it that aren't well known, as well as some very gritty realities. So I thought it might be interesting to take a walk through the city and try and remind myself of the different aspects of the city. And I also thought it would be interesting to take a longer

1

look at Bradford on Avon and see how the two places really compared.

Then it occurred to me that there might be other places that shared a name or some other feature but seemed to have little else in common. Perhaps if I went back to those of them that I had some familiarity with and then explored a partner that I knew less about then I might discover something interesting about how my country was functioning at the moment. More importantly I might have a good time finding out. I offer what follows in the hope that it enables you to share some of that enjoyment.

Bradford

I can't claim that it was the most auspicious of starts. I got off the train in Bradford Yorkshire on a wet day and looked around me. The signs of the city's decline were immediately obvious. This isn't a bustling vibrant city station with people hurrying off to their urgent appointments. It is a station where people seem to listlessly shuffle off the train trying to ignore the signs of decay and dereliction which are all around them. No prizes for best kept station in the country were going to be won here. Lumps of concrete are missing. There is an extraordinarily high brick wall separating the platform from the city centre. Despite all the skill of the Victorian builders it is not a thing of beauty. It has streaks running down it where the cement has leeched or the rain has drawn out a line of uneven filth. As I walked out of the station with the wall hugging close to the pathway I was met with the traditional city greeting. Someone asked me for small change and didn't look like they were about to use it to help to buy themselves a square meal.

But as I started to emerge from the station pathway into the city I made myself look up and there was the first hint that there are some interesting things to be found in the city. The Victorians took great delight in building heavy stone structures with great solid entrance ways and rectangular windows and then finishing them off with a little light flourish at the top. Bradford is full of wonderful examples of this style at its most extreme. The first one I came across was the National Westminster Bank. At ground level it is an intimidating mass of dark stone that looks pretty dull. Look up and you get to see what Victorian architects liked to do when they were set free. They built turrets, they sculpted towers and they played with half digested imitations of Indian palace architecture. In this case they'd gone in for a strange dome that looked more like it belongs in Fatehpur Sikri - the fabulous abandoned palace

3

complex in northern India - than in Bradford. Apart from the cold drizzle and the lack of dazzling sunlight.

The old Wool Exchange just down the road is even more extreme. I decided to take shelter in it for a while. I am not normally given to hanging around in old trade halls on wet days. I had an ulterior motive. This one is a bit different. An astonishing building has been turned into a really nice bookshop. When the Bradford wool merchants were at the height of their success, and people used the phrase "As rich as a Bradford millionaire," it was decided that what the town needed was the best merchants' hall that money could buy. As a result the wool exchange is something to behold. Every inch of its interior has been kitted out to the highest standards and then decorated within an inch of its life. The ceiling is a riot of activity and I knew that with a bit of luck I could sip my coffee from a seat on a balcony whilst taking in a close up view of all that intimate detail. A good bookshop, a coffee and a magnificent building. The day was starting to look up. Even the weather seemed to be improving.

So I wondered back out onto the street and decided to take a look at the town's new pride and joy. They had just finished building a brand new major shopping centre. There aren't many places in the country where the opening of a soulless shopping complex is celebrated with quite so much enthusiasm as it was in Bradford. Then again there can't be too many places where a major part of the city centre gets knocked down and then you have to wait ten years for anyone to start building something in its place. In 2004 when the buildings were demolished it was thought that a modern shopping experience was exactly what the city needed to regenerate itself. Then the developers discovered that it wasn't easy to persuade major retailers to open shops in a city centre where no one seemed to have much money. The owners of the site looked again at their calculations and realised that they were going to have to wait until the profit and loss equation looked a bit more promising. They waited a long time. For ten years the hole in the city centre sat there becoming a symbol of how hard it was to regenerate anything in Bradford. As delay followed delay a malaise settled over the rest of the shops in the city. Many closed down and as they did so more and more people decided to travel to Leeds for their shopping or to buy online. It began to look as if a great hunking empty space which no one was prepared to develop would become a permanent feature of the city. They even had time to turn it into a rather sad and aimless park. Now, finally, the dream had been achieved. In place of a dreary patch of grass there was a bright and shiny new consumer experience.

I have to say I think I preferred the park. Within minutes of entering the closed in streets of neon lighting and desiccated air I began to feel depressed by the whole experience. There are people who like shopping and find it a peaceful and enjoyable recreation. It cheers them up no end to go out and search for a bargain and to come home with something that brightens up their wardrobe. Unfortunately, it has the opposite impact on me. All those sharp lights and primary colours showing off products to their best effect simply make me feel a bit alienated and miserable. I even found myself getting annoyed by what was on offer. Bradford is a city where you can eat astonishingly high-quality food for not very much money. So I thought that the shopping centre food hall might have cashed in on a little of that potential. I could not have been more wrong. There was a Mexican restaurant where no Mexican would have wanted to eat. There was a Chinese restaurant offering food the like of which I never saw anywhere in China. There was a Burger King and a Subway. Authentic Southern American food was also on offer. Provided you didn't mind it being fried chicken from the Colonel's legendary recipe. What you couldn't get was a decent curry. Or any Eastern European specialities. Somehow they had managed to build a shopping centre in one of the most ethnically diverse parts of the country and totally failed to reflect that in either the restaurants or the shops. They were the same old, same old that you can find everywhere else in the country. It was a formula that seemed to be doing very good business. Which shows how much I know about selling to the British shopping public. So I was very pleased for the city that the place had finally been finished and was proving successful but I wanted to get out of it as quickly as possible.

Walking out of the other side took me almost instantly into a completely different world. One minute you are in an airless enclosed street of shops that could be found in an airport lounge almost anywhere in the world. The next you are in one of the oldest parts of the city in a district known as Little Germany. The Westfield Centre is all about the modern shopping experience. It is full of plastic and packaging and is busy doing its bit to bring people back into the city. Little Germany is all about history. It is made up of good old-fashioned structures, dark heavy stone, and narrow streets. It is about as genuinely authentic as you can get. It was virtually empty. In most other places a heritage of 150 year old buildings that have remained largely untouched and unspoiled would be a riot of activity and full of small bars and restaurants enticing you in to explore. I had most of Little Germany to myself. Authenticity wasn't selling desperately well just at the moment.

Efforts had been made to brighten up the area. A few buildings had been turned into office blocks or community art centres. They didn't seem to be doing that well and there weren't enough of them to fight off the overall aura of decline and neglect. Once Bradford was so rich and successful that people left Germany and emigrated to Bradford so that they could take advantage of the vibrant business atmosphere. So many Germans and Jews came here that they built an entire business quarter and used their contacts to sell high quality mass produced Bradford textiles around the world. The town sucked money from the pockets of consumers and wool from the backs of sheep to such an extent that most of the nearby Dales countryside was stripped of arable farms and lost its few remaining upland trees so that more and more sheep could be reared to supply the demands of the factories. Many of those who lost their jobs working on farms ended up using up their lives working hour after hour in the dull interiors of the heavy factories and warehouses that dominate Little Germany. Their work was organised and new machines were so effectively deployed that the factory owners could undercut the price and beat the quality of textiles produced anywhere in the world and so the factories got bigger and more successful and became increasingly specialised. Bradford grew at an astonishing pace. In 1801 there were only 13,264 people living in Bradford. It went up to 103,778 by 1851. From a village to a city in fifty years. By that time there were 382,334 spindles and 17,642 looms for them to work on. [1]

All that is left of this vibrant industry now is the shells of the buildings and no matter how much effort had been put in to try and reuse and revive them it has proved impossible to rid the area of the feeling that something important has gone. It isn't charming or uplifting to walk through this decaying industrial and commercial legacy. It is all a bit depressing. The tall, intimidating lines of warehouse and factory windows and the narrow streets left me with a feeling of walking through an abandoned landscape. Vibrant crowded streets of people hurrying to work are a thing of the past. There is just a sensation of trudging through an empty and declining part of the city where the potential for something more successful has been half-heartedly tried and the money has run out before it has had much impact. So I wandered off into the nearby Cathedral.

Bradford isn't exactly the kind of place most people think of as a Cathedral City. Nevertheless is has a very nice one that is
[1] Bradford, David James, Ryburn, 1990 pages 48 and 32.

genuinely old. A significant amount of the structure dates back to 1458 and the whole building has a very homely feel to it. Some cathedrals seem to have been built with the intention of dominating the individual and putting you into your place. You are being told very firmly that you are a small irrelevant spec of humanity and you had jolly well better bow down to a God that can manage to construct something quite this magnificent. Bradford's cathedral feels like it has been built to house you comfortably whilst you get on with the job of getting in touch with your spiritual side or more probably sitting there waiting patiently for some relative to be christened, married or buried. That might explain why the Royalist took against the place in the civil war. All those self made men and women trying to decide for themselves what way they wanted to worship wouldn't have gone down well with the Cavaliers. So there is a plaque on the wall telling us that they laid siege to the Cathedral twice. Fortunately the roundheads hung enough woolpacks from the tower to ensure that the blows of the royalist cannon fire simply thudded into nice soft absorbent fleeces and did no serious damage to the building. Personally I don't possess much of a spiritual side but even as a good atheist I was grateful their cannonballs hadn't knocked it down and I could sit in comfort and admire the beautiful stained glass windows.

I found myself sitting next to another of the plaques recording important events in the church's history. This one was a bit different to the norm. Instead of venerating some long dead affluent donor it commemorated one of the many waves of immigrants that have arrived here. It turns out that in 1983 the city was celebrating both 40 years of the existence of an Anti Bolshevik Block of Nations and 20 years of a Captive Nations Committee under the leadership of one Yaroslav Stetsko. The history behind these grand words is a fascinating one. During the Second World War the Nazis captured Ukraine. Millions of brave Ukrainians fought and died resisting the invasion of what was then the Soviet Union. Quite a few collaborated and welcomed the invaders with salt and bread or even volunteered to fight alongside the Nazis. They thought that nothing could be worse than the famine they had just lived through as a result of cruel and incompetent forced collectivisation of the land. The behaviour of the Nazis quickly demonstrated how naive that was as Jews, Communists, gypsies, gays and anyone who was a touch too argumentative got rounded up and shot in huge numbers. The Nazis also proceeded to march into each and every village and demand that the mayor supply them with an army of "guest" workers to send back to the munitions factories in Germany. Those who were chosen weren't willing volunteers. They were ripped out of their villages knowing very well that one word of protest might be enough to bring about something much more unpleasant.

At the end of the Second World War any of these forced labourers who ended up on the Eastern side of the iron curtain were treated as if they were little better than active collaborators. Some were shot outright. Many more were deported to labour camps in the East and worked to death. Not surprisingly some of those who were fortunate enough to end up in the West weren't that keen on going back home. They ended up in some surprising places and one of them was Bradford. At the age of 19 Vera Smereka left a small village in the Ukraine because her father was told to supply one member of his family as a guest worker or get shot alongside the Jews who were being regularly taken out to the local ravine. She didn't set foot in her village again for thirty six years and settled down to the life of an exile in Bradford.[2] She was part of a significant Ukrainian community that has been in Bradford ever since the war finished and here on the side of the church wall was the evidence of how strongly that community had felt about their exile.

---

[2] Vera Smereka, The Girl from Ukraine, Contraflow Media, 2008.

I came out of the church and headed off through the town centre in the direction of streets where a much better-known Bradford immigrant community can be found. I wanted to head to Manningham and track down the site of the streets where anger over an attempt at a march through the city by 21st century bigots had triggered some very nasty riots in 2001. The route there took me past what must be the most spectacular Town Hall in the country. A modern civic construction would be done on the cheap and result in a set of very boring rectangular shapes being constructed out of concrete, steel and glass. The Victorians preferred to make a statement. They wanted everyone to know that their town was important and so the place from which it was to be governed was built with the clear intention of making sure no one could possibly forget that. Their Town Hall is a genuine masterpiece. It was built in 1873 but feels like something that would have been created if you had let an arts and crafts enthusiast loose and told them to create the building of their dreams. The architects had obviously set out with the intention of enjoying themselves and, with Bradford at the height of its success, budget restrictions clearly weren't too much of a concern. As soon as the designers had drawn a shape once they seemed to have got bored with that idea and tried to figure out how the next part of the building could be a little bit different and a little bit better. So they had played games with the roofline. They had experimented with window shapes. They had shown off with imposing doorways. And then they had thrown in a few turrets, arches and columns in case anyone thought they weren't trying hard enough. Variety and style had been created at every opportunity. So had detailed decoration. The result was a fabulous building that knocks spots off the more mundane structure of the Houses of Parliament which was put up just a touch earlier.

In an attempt to show the building off to best effect the city fathers had recently cleared a huge area of the centre of the city and created a square in which they'd put some fountains for children to play in on hot days. There wasn't anyone paddling today but the central square did its job. It provided excellent views of the city hall and of the fantastic Alhambra theatre. Unfortunately, it also provided equally excellent views of the brutalist structures of the buildings occupied by the local law courts and of the decaying splendours of a huge disused cinema. I gave both of those a miss and headed up the hill towards Manningham.

On the way you quickly acquire a real feel for how much decline and neglect the city has suffered. I went past a closed down Department Store on a dismal busy road that seemed to have been rammed through the heart of the city by some over enthusiastic late 60s town planner. In the distance I could see street after street of decaying factory buildings and the odd high rise flat mixed in with efforts to revive the whole thing by building up the University and College quarter. I went past a burned-out pub next door to a seedy strip club, a number of pound shops and pawnbrokers and spotted plenty of places where bushes were growing out of the upper floors of buildings which should have been national treasures but were suffering serious decay. But the advantage of neglected areas is that you also come across some deeply eccentric places where you can find things that are much more interesting than you would come across in a brightly lit shopping centre. At the top of the hill I discovered a collection of music shops. In Bradford you can still find vinyl records and second hand CDs for sale that don't come with designer prices. You can get a recycled banjo or accordion or indeed almost any other musical instrument you might care to want to find. I also found a drum centre where young musicians could bash away at some very high-quality equipment and imagine that they and their band were going to make it out of here one day.

There is also an excellent local market. If the new shopping centre suffered from a lack of authenticity and didn't seem to reflect the diversity of the local community then there is no worry about that in the market. It is a foodies delight. You can get obscure ingredients from any of the city's ethnic minority groups. If you want to go Eastern European then you can get any amount of pickled fish, smoked meat or flavoured vodka. If you fancy West Indian then you can expand your knowledge of bottles of obscure spiced ketchups and interesting ways to use coconuts. You can get Middle Eastern food that you won't find in a posh restaurant in Kensington but you will find on the streets of Afghanistan. And, of course, you can also find one of the finest displays of vegetables for 'Indian' cooking that you'll come across this side of Pakistan. All this is mixed in with a selection of totally traditional Yorkshire produce. If you want to make up a recipe for black pudding korma then this is probably the place to come. I have been round quite a few bazaars in places like Marakesh, Istanbul and Aswan. These days rather too many of those seem to have become pastiches of themselves and to simply be offering products that the tourists might be fool enough to pay too much for. This was a genuine working bazaar doing brisk business offering things that the locals wanted and all the better for it.

There seem to be two different shopping experiences in Bradford. In the centre you can experience the same sort of shops you'll find anywhere else in the country. On the edges all that changes as you approach the areas where recent immigrants live alongside the Pakistani and Bangladeshi communities who came in the 50s and the descendants of those who poured into Bradford to work in the factories and never made their fortune. Instead of this producing nothing but dirt poor corner shops what you actually find is that this is where the top end jewellers, clothing shops, bakers and shoe shops have chosen to set up business. If you like your gold to have a particularly high karat then this is the place to come. I counted five different high-class goldsmiths doing a roaring trade on the street where much of the action in the Bradford riots took place. Instead of heading into the city centre to do their shopping many of the local residents prefer to use shops that grew out of their community and, as a consequence, some very successful shops have gathered together on obscure backstreets to meet their needs. So if you are getting ready for a posh Asian wedding then you can get your gold jewellery, buy a magnificent sari, spend ages deciding which designer shoes to wear, and order a cake that will look totally spectacular all in the comfort of shops that are yards from where you live. Or perhaps where you used to live if you have earned enough to get out to the suburbs but can't find the right stores there.

I don't want to give the wrong impression here. The streets that saw a huge outpouring of anger and where rioters burned down buildings have not been replaced by wall to wall designer Asian shopping centres. The area is still very poor and very deprived and you don't have to look at street after street of decay and the night shift taxis parked outside of run down houses for very long before understanding what the root cause of the riots really were. Nevertheless, there is a change. There are pockets around the city where you can see signs that parts of the local community have done alright and have money to spend. Many of them want to spend it in their own way in their own community and so they have established a ring of places around the city where you can find some very high-end products on sale in some very glitzy shops.

It is just as well that there are moments of brightness because walking the inner-city suburbs of Bradford is not an uplifting experience. Again and again you come across buildings that were once rather posh but aren't any more. There are, of course, terraces of back to backs. But that isn't the norm in this part of Bradford. Mostly the poorer areas of Bradford consist of huge houses that once were homes for clerks from the warehouses or lecturers from the Mechanics Institute but are now ideal for large extended families. There are grand crescents - with piles of rubbish dumped outside them. There are homes built in the same spirit as the city hall where every opportunity has been taken to construct something grand and imposing. You can find a mattress outside them on a bit of neglected scrubland that was once a garden. External timbers are cracking and paint is peeling off the outside of buildings that really ought to be listed. There are signs outside some of the larger and most magnificent buildings advertising dirt poor doss houses in several different Eastern European languages. Poverty doesn't sit well with either the buildings or the people. Everyone who past me seemed to shuffle by without much sense of purpose.

This is the real heart of the problem with Bradford. It can be a fantastic community. It has lots of really interesting and unusual aspects to it. But there is no getting away from the fact that far too many people in the city are genuinely very poor and have been for far too long. Buildings which would have been renovated within an inch of their lives and areas which would have been spotted as ideal for gentrification in many other parts of the country have not been touched for years here. There just isn't enough money and there is just too much to tackle. The city's schools are full of great people doing really good work. After years of battling against the odds to get the kids some kind of qualifications and then discovering they are towards the bottom of the league tables once again there is a real temptation for the best teachers to give up the battle and move to work in a place where the job is easier. Successful parents from the Asian community are tempted to follow them and get their kids into nicer schools in the suburbs. There are some signs of pockets of success in Bradford and it is possible that communities will prefer to stay there and build on it. There is also real disadvantage and a long history of people trying to move out of the city as soon as they can to get to nicer places which don't smell of neglect.

The Office of National Statistics reports that there are parts of Bradford where 60% of the population live off less than 60% of the median income in the country. This needs a bit of translation. The median income is the commonest one in the country and if you pick 60% of that level then you can pretty much guarantee than anyone below that will be poor. If you live in the wrong part of Bradford then that kind of poverty is something that you aspire to achieve. Only 40% of local people make enough money to creep over the most widely used definition of poverty. The majority live off less. Some of them a lot less. And, of course, you can see that on the streets. There isn't just one small area of poverty in Bradford. It stretches for miles.

Eventually, as you continue walking out of the city you start to emerge from the poorest areas. At the boundary between the two I found myself walking into Cartwright Hall where the wealthy home of an industrialist has been turned into an art gallery and some very nice gardens. Then I walked past Bradford Grammar School, an imposing structure housing a very large and successful private school that draws in the children of the well off from miles around. If I'd gone on a bit further I'd have ended up in the model village of Saltaire where the philanthropist Titus Salt built high quality homes, educational facilities, and parks for his workers. Then he slightly spoiled much of the good will that generated by insisting that they couldn't have a pub and would be well advised to make sure they were seen regularly at the very imposing church that he thought it more suitable to provide. Nevertheless, he built a huge and very successful factory and an equally successful community that has now been transformed into a desirable suburb. After a long decline and a period of closure his factory was eventually converted with great success. Inside it you can have an excellent lunch, explore the designer cook shop, study the most impressive display of local boy David Hockney's work anywhere in the world, buy yourself some jewellery, and browse a few books whilst you take in the architecture. You can even earn your living in a high-tech electronics company or buy yourself a top end mountain bike or an expensive carpet. Bradford doesn't do middle class often but when it does it carries it off quite well.

I didn't quite make it to Saltaire or to the suburbs on this occasion. After trudging through a couple of miles of inner city deprivation I had run out of energy and enthusiasm for exploration. I got as far as a rather sad little station called Frizinghall and headed back home. Bradford Yorkshire is a fascinating city for anyone with even the remotest interest in social history but it was pretty clear to me that it wasn't going to get to the centre stage of any tourist's agenda any time soon.

****

Bradford on Avon gets tourists in droves. It is a couple of hundred miles away from its namesake in distance and a lot more on every other measure you might care to come up with. Bradford the city has its share of people who care about it but no one would claim that it is an easy and comfortable place. That is exactly what Bradford on Avon is. This is where you come to if you want to find a charming little tea shop, nestled beside a gently flowing river. The buildings are made out of the same golden stone that helps to make nearby Bath look so very fine. It works even better here. The streets climb a steep hill almost as soon as you cross the river and so you get a clear sight of terrace after terrace of beautiful houses each one marking out the next stage of the rise. It makes for a quite magnificent panorama. Bradford on Avon gives posh a good name.

I arrived by car. So, it seemed, did a lot of other people. It isn't easy finding a place to park in a town full of rather nice motor vehicles and even nicer houses. The tourist car park fills up very quickly and you have to pick a quiet day and get there early in the morning or be in luck if you want to find a spot that is as easy walk into town. My route took me over the thirteenth century bridge that spans the Avon at a place which looks very likely to have been the original broad ford that produced the name. The stone has aged attractively, having become softened with time. It has taken on a gently weathered appearance and it seemed tempting to touch so I leaned over the parapet and took a long look at the river sliding past. The water is astonishingly clear and as a result long strands of weed stretch out in line with the current and move calmly back and forth with the flow. It took a minute to get the eye in but then all of a sudden I started to spot the shapes of fish lingering in the faster flowing parts in the hope that some food would be washed their way. Every now and then one of them would tire of waiting in their current spot and decide that it was time to give a flick of the tail and see whether things were more promising in the channel just alongside. It was done with such economy of effort that the trout looked to be living a very easygoing life.

Just across the bridge and into the town much the same seemed to be true of the local people. This is the sort of place where no local can walk down to the shops without needing to stop several times to catch up with some friend and neighbour. You have to allow not just enough time to make your purchases but more importantly to talk. Many of the people here appear to have lived in the locality for a very long time and to enjoy the opportunity to share the small experiences of life with each other. I found myself constantly having to stop to dodge little groups of friends who were too caught up in conversation to notice that they were blocking the pavement. They seemed well dressed, well off folks who were living with sufficient ease to pause and enjoy the company of their neighbours.

But Bradford on Avon can be deceptive. It may now be full of tea shops and people spending a pleasant afternoon, a comfortable retirement or an easy life. That wasn't always the way things have been. The town was founded on textile mills every bit as much as the other place named after a broad ford was. The difference is partly one of timing. Bradford on Avon had its boom and bust a lot earlier than Bradford Yorkshire. It has come out the other side of it with sufficient time for the scars to soften and to look like interesting features instead of raw wounds. The Avon valley was a great place to raise sheep with the steep rounded oolitic limestone slopes providing plenty of lush grazing but not being ideal for arable crops. With a steady supply of water power from a fast flowing river it made sense to make up woollen garments close to the raw material and all that water also made for a very convenient resource when it came to cleaning wool or tanning hides. Consequently the woollen industry in this area was a roaring success from early times and especially so from around 1650 to 1800. Many of the merchants and manufacturers did very well for themselves and were able to build some very grand houses out of the proceeds. The same oolitic limestone that made it very convenient to farm sheep also made for a particularly beautiful colour of building stone. Down the road in Bath it has become famous for giving the whole city a warm and gentle appearance. Here the homes acquired a more lived in appearance that is more natural and to my eye even more attractive. Even the old workers' cottages now look highly desirable.

But back in the seventeen hundreds there was nothing genteel about the appearance and the stench of Bradford on Avon. Textiles can be a smelly and a dirty business, particularly if there is a large dye works in the town, and that was one of the most important businesses in this busy early industrial town. I once happened upon the tanning and dye works in the back streets of Marrakesh. It was an experience that has stuck with me. Mainly for the smell. A mixture of goats urine, fullers earth and dyestuffs isn't the easiest thing to forget. It got to the back of your nostrils with a insistent determination. It also managed to penetrate every corner of the streets around the works with an impressively pungent aroma that seemed to be soaking into your body as easily as it was into the hides. Great vats of animal skins lay in tubs where a mixture of processes were being inflicted upon them. Some people were occupied by stirring garments in a liquid of a vicious colour. Nearby desperately poor downtrodden workers were standing up to their knees so that they could consume their working lives in treading up and down to soften leather. A clumsy wooden contraption was being turned so that it repeatedly beat fabric into the desired condition. As a consequence a great deal of noise accompanied the smell.

It is therefore not hard to imagine what the Avon must have looked like downstream from the dye works. It would have run filthy from the different coloured vegetable stains. With an additional odour of collected and stored human urine. Then for good measure there would have been the run-off from the homes gathered on the river banks that lacked a decent sewage system. And the odd bit of early industrial waste would have been included in the mix. As the town's local historian describes it:

'Bradfordians relied on rain and the town's many natural watercourses to wash garbage, horse dung and cattle droppings down to the river, itself already looked upon by the inhabitants and industry as a sewer provided free of charge by bountiful nature.'[3]

What looks now like a pristine trout river that has never been messed with would have been heavily polluted by one of the worst industries out. Its banks would have been lined by factories every bit as ugly as the early ones in Bradford. In winter there would have been a significant degree of air pollution coming from the burning of the Somerset coal that was first used to keep everyone warm and then later to power the machinery. The fumes would have sunk back down into the valley on a cold day as a temperature inversion trapped

[3] Bradford Upon Avon Past & Present, Harold Fassnidge, p126 (Ex Libris Press, 2007)

the smoke. The big difference from the city of Bradford is that few of the factories along the Avon prospered after the leap to coal fired technology, partly because they lost out the race to industrialise most efficiently to their Yorkshire competitor. Yorkshire coal was cheap and conveniently nearer to hand for the northern Bradford woollen manufacturers. Yorkshire wool was available in greater quantities and there were better connections to the main markets. So the one town gradually got more of the business and the other less. Bradford Yorkshire became the best place to ply the trade and the factories there started to grow in number, get bigger, specialise more and produce even more efficiently. The consequence for the Wiltshire town was inevitable. Throughout the nineteenth century the textile industry declined in the Avon version of Bradford every bit as rapidly as it grew in the Yorkshire variant.

In 1815 there were thirty wool manufacturers in Bradford on Avon producing 678 ends of broad cloth. Twenty-three years later there were only three left making 144 ends. In 1840 there were 367 handlooms in the town. Half of them were idle because of the fierce competition from well-equipped factories up north. [4] At the time it must have felt like a disaster. They probably cast an envious eye on those folk who happened to be fortunate enough to live in their more successful namesake. In the 1791 the out of work former employees in one of the workshops got so angry about the loss of their previous livelihood that they besieged a factory. Joseph Phelps the factory owner saved his life by the simple strategy of superior armoury and brutal indifference to the consequences of using it. He fired on the mob and killed three of them. There were still decades of hard times ahead for the local industry and I suspect few of the families of the laid off workers would have seen any positives to the decline. Nor would they have been entirely comforted by any early talk of

---

[4] Ibid, p 40

the benefits of the hidden hand of the market and the inevitability of change.

These days losing out in the race to be the most successful manufacturing location in the industrial revolution doesn't look such a bad thing. Bradford Yorkshire's gain has turned out to be a very mixed blessing indeed and Bradford on Avon's loss hasn't turned out so bad. Instead of finding that every inch of the town was eaten up by thrustingly successful new industry and commerce the southern town moved ahead at a much slower pace. Both places have a legacy of fantastic buildings left over from those who made money in the industrial revolution and before. In Yorkshire there are so many of them that the vast majority have proved impossible to preserve. Building after building is crumbling into the ground and stands as a neglected accusation. Others have been knocked down to make way for sterile 1960s throughways, tired supermarket car parks or attempts to create office block developments that have also failed. On the banks of the Avon they were left with just enough disused factories to be able to turn them into attractive apartment blocks looking out over a river that has had time to recover its composure. They were able to preserve their heritage buildings converting them into stylish retirement homes and the like instead of being left with such an intimidating surplus of great buildings and so few wealthy residents that the vast majority of them fell into serious disrepair.

Bradford on Avon came out of the industrial revolution as a slightly forgotten location. A place where the steep sided valleys made it hard to create massive industrial units but a good location to establish a rather fine residence. As a consequence, it is now a joy to walk around. It has something remaining from every era from Roman through to modern and it has been built in a bewildering variety of styles. Yet there is a coherence to the place that works. Because so many of the buildings have been made with the same stone you have the

21

feeling that they all belong together even when they were constructed at very different times for very different purposes. Indeed the variety of building styles is part of the fun of the place. It is rare for two buildings to be identical and so as I walked away from the town centre and started to explore the back street terraces there were plenty of interesting little details to look at in each of the houses the I passed.

I chose one of the terraces high up on the hill almost at random and walked along it. The land was so steep that the builders had decided that there wasn't room for a road and had settled for just putting a small path right outside the front doors. The houses were then dug into the hillside leaving no room out the back. In the absence of any possibility of a proper back garden a little plot of land was provided out front, just across the public footpath. Passers by now walk along a thin pavement separating local residents from their gardens. Anyone living here who wants to sit out and enjoy the view is forced to cross that right of way. This seemed to me to have accidently turned into a major gain for the local residents. Instead of being shut up in their own private little space they have been gently encouraged to conduct a rather more public life. You could see the results as you walked past their front door. The residents seemed to be happily talking to each other and the fine displays of pot plants outside each front door indicated that they had been determined to outdo their neighbours with their gardening efforts. Each little plot of land seemed to have been turned into a display of fascinatingly different plants and designs where the residents could sit and look out above the roofs of the terrace below and down across the whole of the river valley. Far in the distance there was an ancient white horse on a ridge of hills. Down at the valley bottom you could make out the river sliding through a park towards the refurbished retirement homes that had once been factories. Up here on the hill a lot of time and care had gone into each and every garden and as you walked along the path people greeted you easily as if they were happy to see you enjoying the sight of their handiwork. They were clearly working on generous land where most things prospered and grew with ease but equally clearly a lot of time and skill had gone into making sure their little bit of land was a pleasure to sit in. This was the sort of environment where things grow easily and where gardeners needed to devote a lot more time and effort on trying to cut back and shape plants that wanted to run out of control rather than struggling to get new plants established.

For the visitor the result was simply delightful. You could walk along the little path in front of the houses and find pleasurable things to look at in every direction. To your right there were wonderful little houses made of ageing stone that had crumbled in places. This made the individuality of the very walls of the buildings worth studying and the same was even more true of each of the details of the roof, the windows, the guttering or the doorways. Gnarled branches of long established climbing trees crawled their way across some of the frontages and the wisteria was in flower giving a gorgeous scent along with an abundance of blue flowers. If you chose to look to the left as you walked you could enjoy discovering what treasures the owner of the next house had hidden away in their own little bit of garden. Every now and then a tiny alleyway ran off up or down the hillside to make it easy to pay a visit to the neighbours in the terrace above or below. Trees from the gardens hung over the edge of the walls of these alleyways and they rambled erratically upwards in ways that seemed designed to encourage you to wander up that particular alleyway so that you could see what was just round the corner.

I resisted the temptation until I'd got to the end of the row and was rewarded by coming across a lovely little Chapel that had once housed a community of pilgrims and had some evidence of being built on Anglo Saxon origins. Then I worked my way down the terraces and found myself inside an even smaller and older church built just above the flood plain of the river. An awful lot of effort seemed to have gone into creating a very small space of worship. It felt like fifty Saxons would have filled the place easily but back in the first millennium that was probably the best part of the population of the town. Crossing the river took me to an old tithe barn which showed that the middle ages must have been a lot more prosperous. A huge high empty structure with an enormously powerful set of roof beams had been built just to store the grain that people needed to offer up as their share of the taxes. However irksome it must have been for local farmers to have that much of their hard work taken away, it represented strong evidence that those farmers must have been doing very well indeed to be able to produce this kind of surplus. The town had clearly flourished in the days when agriculture was the most important activity

It was flourishing again now and this was producing its own problems for local residents. Instead of struggling to get by in crumbling decay on streets that had seen serious riots the residents of Bradford on Avon were clearly blessed with some very pleasant surroundings which gave off a real sense of community. This was a place with a history that easily generates a sense of security and belonging. I walked along the river bank for a while and then back along the canal and got the same sense of people enjoying themselves in nice surroundings that I had encountered in the whole of the town. Couples were out walking their designer dogs accompanied by well dressed children. Some were out riding bikes or jogging. Most were just strolling with their kids. I stopped at a wild-life pond that had been recently put in and already it was occupied by hundreds of newts swimming confidently around in full view of the local children. Parents were happily pointing them out to their offspring. It you had the opportunity to bring your kids up in this kind of environment then you would want them to be able to stay on and enjoy it and you'd have every reason to be confident that they would be very reluctant to leave.

And therein lies perhaps the major problem for this Bradford. Because it is so desirable it is also very expensive. Local kids will need to be doing very well indeed it they want to become local adults living in their own home. At times the place feels like you are living in something out of Jane Austin. Which is great if all you want is to look at beautiful surroundings. If you want to purchase your little place in this apparent paradise you need a great deal of money. That isn't necessarily very easy to do for anyone has only just joined the local job market. Especially if they are saddled with heavy student loans to pay off. So a lot of local young people end up with a choice of either living with their parents long into their adult life or moving out to somewhere less attractive but cheaper or offering more prosperous employment. The town is consequently quite elderly and the society is starting to resemble Jane Austin's in ways that are considerably less attractive than the architecture. For the vast majority of local young people the only ways they can carry on living here are to either benefit from an early inheritance or live under the grace and favour of the older generation. We seem to have gone back to the days where the first thing a young person needs to know before planning a long term relationship is what their potential partner's expectations are and where it is very difficult indeed to bridge some of the class barriers.

Visiting Bradford on Avon so soon after walking around the gritty streets of Bradford in Yorkshire I couldn't help wondering what would happen if anyone swapped places. A cultural exchange programme would shock most of the residents of either town to the core. The two places seem to exist in their own bubbles of reality that have almost nothing in common with each other. Take a resident from the Wiltshire town and ask them to live for a week in the Yorkshire city and you suspect that they would find the experience deeply traumatic. Reverse the process and I suspect that the participants might enjoy it rather more. But it might very well make them wonder if they could ever succeed in breaking out of the one place and earning enough to live in the other. Walking round the namesakes I felt like we had created a country in which great chunks of our population is utterly unaware of the way another set of people live their lives. One set of Bradford people is unlikely to have the faintest idea how hard it is to succeed in education or at work in a tough inner-city environment. The vast majority of the residents of the much poorer city have little opportunity to witness what the wealthier community values and enjoys, or to feel any real connection with the aspiration to achieve anything remotely as comfortable.

This kind of extreme contrast does not make for shared experiences and shared understanding. I set off next for a place of equally sharp contrasts – this time between an urban and a rural environment.

Clapham

A little over twenty years ago I left London and moved to a small village on the edge of the Yorkshire Dales. For much of my time in London I had lived in the vicinity of Clapham in a flat facing onto the three lane highway that comes over Wandsworth Bridge and heads off into the suburbs. If I wanted to take the train then I would walk down the hill to Clapham Junction and enter the busiest station in Europe. Two thousand trains a day pass through Clapham Junction with over half of them stopping. It has 17 platforms and, in the morning, it feels like every one of them is filled with people heading somewhere urgently. Even if most of them look a bit bored.

A few weeks after we moved we decided to take a trip out into the Dales to go for a walk. I looked at a map to see if I could find somewhere interesting and I discovered that there was another Clapham with its own station. In any one direction five trains stop there in a day. Not many people get off and those that do have a long walk before they get to the village. They built the station down in the main valley to speed up through journey times and cut down on cost. The village is a mile away up nearer the hills. Sheltering from the wind. We decided to take the car.

It was worth the trip. We parked easily enough. It was autumn and out of the main tourist season so we found a spot right in the centre of the village next to a small stream that is closed in by dry stone walls. As soon as we got out of the car and turned off the engine we were immediately struck by the sound of ... well by the sound of not very much. Some wind going through the trees. A touch of gentle babbling was coming from the brook. A couple of birds called occasionally. And that was about it. The contrast with the constant noise of London traffic could not have been more extreme. At the time we weren't able to walk more than a couple of miles because we had our son with us. He had reached the stage where he was too heavy to carry and had developed some of his own critical faculties. He used them to be suitably critical of our plan to walk him up one of the highest hills in England on legs that were not even half as long as those of his parents'. Yet even on that brief trip it was evident that this was one of the best walking spots in the country and we had to come back. Since then I have returned many times to the small quiet Clapham and once or twice to the busy noisy one.

This time I picked a dry warm day to go back to the village. The best walk starts from the corner grocery shop and heads in one simple direction. Upwards. For a couple of hundred yards I walked alongside the beck which at this time of year, after several dry days, was coming gently off the mountainside. The bed of the stream is dotted with chunks of stone that have been swept down on days when the weather is more violent. There are quite a lot of those. I stood on the quaint old stone footbridge that led over the stream and looked down upon them. The water was gurgling along nicely and separated itself as it hit each stone into a constantly shifting pattern of light and movement. The stones had settled into the river bank and looked confident and secure, as if nothing could ever shift them from their rightful place. Yet every one of them had been tumbled down here at some point in history by the sheer force of nothing more than water.

As you walk up the path towards the hills there is a little platform that has been put by the side of the stream to help you pause and take in the view of a waterfall. The cascade looks picture perfect, seemingly falling just the right distance before hitting a ledge, swirling around stylishly and then falling again onto the next obstacle and pouring over it down towards the village. It all looks a bit too well designed to be true. There is a reason for this. It isn't a natural feature and it was indeed carefully designed. At great expense by a member of the Farrer family.

Clapham is small enough that one family has been able to dominate its history and put its mark on the landscape and the architecture in the way that no one could do in a place as large and complex as Clapham in London. The first building that you see if you alight at the station in Yorkshire is an impressive substantial home called Farrer Lodge. It is only the Lodge you understand. The main house and grounds are around a mile away, above the village. The family weren't short of cash. They sold land to the North Western railway in 1847 that was worth £2,881 and picked up another £2,101 from sale of land to the Settle Carlisle railway before 1880.[5] These kinds of sums were not to be sneezed at in those days. Carefully and sensibly managed they were enough to enable a family to live very well and indulge a few pleasures. Especially if you had a successful legal and financial business.

The pleasure which the family seemed to enjoy the most was doing interesting things to their land and property. The tradition had been begun by James and James William Farrer who spent over 30 years at the start of the nineteenth century on a radical design and makeover which included creating their own lake and finishing it off with the over perfect cascade that I was looking at admiringly. It didn't come cheap. According to their most famous descendant, Reginald Farrer:

"one of my ancestors was lured by degrees, on the first pretence of making a few fish pools, into so damming up the stream at the valley's exit as to make the whole glen one broad long lake. A noble work: and when the bills came in, he was filled with shame and terror, and put them all in the fire. So that posterity has no notion of his lavishness." [6]

---

[5] Sarah Mason, The Ingleborough Estate, in Reginald Farrer, Dalesman, Plantsman, Gardener, (Chase Production, 1991) p85
[6] Reginald Farrer, In a Yorkshire Garden, (1909 reprinted by Theophrastus 1978) p267

This is typical of Reginald Farrer's writing style. The most famous member of the Farrer family liked a joke. He also liked a lot of other things. Plants, travel, strong opinions, walking, rock gardens and his own company. He became one of the great plant collectors and a best-selling writer on horticulture, travel and religion, producing nineteen books and a host of articles for magazines.

I rather suspect that Reginald Farrer didn't get much fun out of his early childhood. A speech impediment was not the ideal inheritance for a little boy in a tough Yorkshire village in 1880. If he was forced to spend a great deal of time in his own company, then it proved a blessing in disguise. He developed a serious interest in botany. These days when you say that someone has an interest in a topic it can easily mean that they have looked up the subject on the internet and posted a video on Facebook. Reginald was just a little more serious about it than that. He studied in Oxford. He climbed the Alps in pouring rain and snow to find and collect rare species. He went to Japan to study rock gardens and to Sri Lanka to investigate the way chaotic jungle plants invaded the ancient ruins of one of the proudest civilisations in early history. Then he went to China and Burma. He produced a series of great books about his travels and his garden which are gloriously well written and are often very funny indeed. Provided you don't mind wading through a long series of Latin plant names before you get to the punch lines. Along the way he became a Buddhist as well as England's leading expert in obscure plants. Searching for those was an interest that obsessed him for his whole life and which gave him huge pleasure. Eventually it killed him. But if you are going to die, and let's face it we all are, there are few better ways than collapsing in upper Burma in the company of a couple of local guides after exploring a gloriously interesting hillside where you think that there might just be a really unusual species of verbena.

Reginald brought some of the plants he liked back to England. Many of them can still be found in pride of place in botanical gardens where they have been carefully labelled and tenderly looked after by experts who know every detail about them from their taxonomic classification to their genetic codes. Quite a few of them are stuck in the grounds of his old family home in Clapham or on the hillside above his ancestor's expensive lake without any labels or anyone really knowing where they are.

As a result you can never be quite sure what the obscure plant is that you have just strolled past as you start to walk upwards out of the village and enter grounds that were once part of the Farrer estate. The land is now managed by volunteers, so you are asked to put a tiny amount towards the upkeep into an honesty box as you pass by. No one checks that you have done so. You pick up a ticket from a machine but there is no ticket inspector. It is simply taken for granted that any reasonable person will put the money into the machine. Then you pass on through up the valley.

You find yourself walking along a path out of Clapham that doesn't look anything like you expect a Yorkshire Dales valley to look. It is managed woodland rather than empty hills given over to sheep. The path goes alongside the edge of a lake that has been created with just the right amount of curves and then bordered by tall specimens of whatever magnificent tree Reginald, or his gloriously profligate ancestors, put there. The valley below you is full of rhododendrons brought straight from the east and then left to go semi wild. Much of the ground on either side of the path through the valley gets full of wild garlic in spring and the smell of what are locally called ransoms is an intense experience.

I was a bit too early for the main show on my walk but even before the season properly began I could catch the first hints of the aroma starting to come through. I came across a folly with a nice arch and a seat which looks like it has been taken straight out of the pages of a Victorian decorator's design booklet. I sat down for a while to enjoy the view. Victorian designers clearly didn't do comfort so I got up again quite quickly. There was something just a touch dark and sinister about some of those plants from the other side of the world that were slowly taking over from the native flora. I felt that if I sat down on my own for a bit too long then one of Reginald's prize specimens would probably put a creeper round my neck, pull me into the undergrowth, and use me for a bit of extra nourishment. It doesn't do to have read John Wyndham's The Day of the Triffids if you have an over active imagination and want to sit still for any length of time in a garden full of obscure botanical treasures.

Eventually I reached the end of the managed area and emerged into more open country. By this point the river valley has closed in quite a bit and either side of the beck there are steep hills. On the floor of the valley there is a thin carpet of grass and herbs trodden down by multitudes of walkers and liberally decorated with sheep droppings. The stream dribbles down across this meadow making a set of small pools which look perfect for paddling children. I put my hand into one of these pools and quickly changed my mind about dangling my feet into the water. Much too cold for childish toes. And for elderly ones. On each side the valley walls rise above you and sharp angular rocks poke out through the tufts of tough grass. Any lingering sensation of being overwhelmed by fiercely growing vegetation quickly left me. The soil here is too thin for even Reginald to have done much with it. Instead the land is now so stark that it begins to feel like you are in perfect ambush territory. It has the kinds of rock outcrop that they used to hide cowboys behind in all those awful wild west programs they were fond of putting on the telly during my youth.

But the valley hides something a lot more interesting than a bad B movie actor trying to work his way up to becoming

President. It contains one of the most spectacular cave systems in Britain and possibly the most beautiful one that is easily accessible on foot. Or at least that is how you can get to them now. When they were discovered in the 1830s the caves here were flooded. Nowadays if we discovered a pristine flooded cave where no human had ever set foot it would almost certainly be the subject of a serious scientific study. It is highly likely that there would have been an entire ecosystem in this lake including fish with no eyes that had developed the ability to live and prosper in a darkened world. That is certainly what is frequently found in similar caves in Central Europe. But back then discoverers didn't bother too much with such awkward details. They blasted away the rubble that was blocking the entrance and got rid of the pesky lake to make way for tourists. As business plans go it was an effective one. The Ingleborough Caves did a roaring trade in the Victorian era as people flocked to see the spectacular sight of complex stalactites & stalagmites reflected in the depths of the remaining pools of water. Even today, when we have all seen the best creations of science fiction worlds that computer enhanced digital imagery can produce, these reflections in the pools still fire the imagination. Water dripping from the limestone roof has fallen on the ground in such unpredictable ways that it has left gloriously eccentric shapes which are then copied in perfect detail onto the surface of still pools by the electric light that now illuminates the caves. Or at least illuminates them until the guides plays their favourite party trick and turn off all the lights for a full minute so that everyone can experience the total darkness of the caves depths.

I gave the caves a miss this time as I had seen them more than once. Shortly after you pass them the walls of the valley start to close in upon you and there is no longer a stream. Far above you it has plunged underground and you are walking along a path that it took way back in the distant past. The bottom of the valley is completely dry now and as it gets narrower and narrower the sides become more gaunt and vertical until you reach a point where there is no path left to walk on at all. Just a scramble route that is marked out by a smoothing on the rocks. It doesn't take any great climbing skills but there are plenty of points where you need to use your hands and to think carefully about the best means to pick your way over the tumbled rocks of what looks like a dry waterfall. I kept my eyes firmly on the ground as I pulled myself up through what had become a steep stony gorge. And then the ground started to flatten out a bit and before I knew it I was out in open country with Ingleborough standing out proudly on the horizon above me. This is what I have always loved about walking around Clapham. You get three kinds of scenery in a relatively short distance. After the wooded managed landscape and the limestone gorge you emerge onto the typical highland countryside of the Yorkshire Dales. Wild moors. Sheep. Rough grass. And wind.

The wind and the cold increased significantly as soon as I emerged from the shelter of the valley and onto the more open countryside. So I didn't hang around to look down into Gaping Gill and strode on past it. There isn't actually much to see from the top of the tallest cavern in the country. It is a genuinely dangerous spot where over curious people have tumbled to their deaths on more than one occasion in quite recent times. All you can see is a rather uninspiring looking sink hole that might lead nowhere much in particular. It is only if you come on the days when the caving clubs have set up a winch and organised things properly that there is much point in approaching the entrance. Then, if you are brave enough and prepared to give them a reasonable donation towards their work, they will dangle you from a wire and let you hang in supreme isolation hundreds of feet above the cave bottom as you are lowered down towards it. I have been offered to opportunity to partake of this experience on more than one occasion. I have always managed to spectacularly bottle it and whenever I have seen the pictures of celebrity TV presenters being filmed on the journey down I have never entirely regretted my more cautious approach. Nice to watch on TV but seriously scary.

The walk up to the top of Ingleborough is seemingly much more straightforward. All it requires is to put one foot in front of the other and for each step to take you a little bit higher than the last one. Unfortunately, you have to do that a great many times. There are rather a lot of steps and it quickly seeks out any gaps in your physical fitness and exposes them ruthlessly. Mine meant that I decided to stop on numerous occasions and pretend that I was merely enjoying the view. So it took a while to get to the top. Along the way there were plenty of opportunities to stare at the intimidating shape of Ingleborough looming above me.

Ingleborough is shaped like a mini Table Mountain. You climb steadily over open rising moorland until you are near the summit. Then there is a sudden steep bit as you hit hard ancient rock that has refused to wear away under the relentless battering of the Yorkshire weather despite millions of years of storms. This layer of Millstone Grit rock looks like a huge slab that has been plonked on the top of the hill and you have to struggle up the side of that hard sandstone slab before you reach the flat top. Once there you discover that the summit area is surprisingly spacious. Back in the iron age people built a low border bank all the way round the edge of the hill and a number of circular buildings on the flat summit. It would have made one hell of a good defensive site but a really cold and unwelcoming place to live. Consequently, modern experts are far from sure what reason iron age folk had for putting quite so much construction work in a spot like this.[7] The lack of certainty leaves ample opportunity for the

---

[7] David Johnson, Ingleborough (Carnegie Publishing, 2008), p109

amateur to speculate. Either there were some seriously scary people around and it was worth sleeping in a horribly cold place to keep away from them or else the locals went up there occasionally for purposes that we don't understand. What the archaeologists call rituals.

My own ritual was to wander about from side to side taking in the different views of the distance. Looking northward I could see nothing but moors and hills all the way to Scotland. It is dramatic stark scenery. The land lies open and the few farm houses that you can see simply seem to increase the sensation of looking out over an empty landscape. There isn't a great deal of human activity to see in the other three directions either. Imposing hills, deep valleys and bare hillsides dominate. There can't be many countries where you can leave behind heavily populated industrial towns and look out over remote almost deserted open countryside as easily as you can in this part of Britain.

For many years I thought that this wild empty landscape was the natural state of affairs and that walking the hills was getting me back into contact with unspoiled nature. Nothing could be further from the truth. This isn't an untouched landscape left alone to be the way that nature created it. Humans have been messing with it for centuries. Looking out over such a huge expanse of open moorland is a great pleasure but it is one that comes at a price. The trees have been stripped away by human activity. Some of the steeper hillsides with the more dramatic rock outcrops are, of course, unlikely to have ever held many trees. The same is true of the places with naturally occurring thin acid soil or where it was permanently soaked. Most of the area was however some form of woodland before humanity came on the scene. The natural flora consists of a mixture of tough short native trees and shrubs that can hold their own in all this wind and rain. There are still patches of it still surviving or deliberately recreated in a few parts of the Dales. Not that I could see any sign of that around here. Standing on the top of Ingleborough it didn't seem to matter which direction I chose to look. The trees had gone. A few isolated plantations of massed ranks of conifers could be spotted. They really only served as a reminder that woodland could have survived here but hasn't. It was like looking at the Brazilian rain forest after the loggers have done their worst. I could see a long way and the views were fantastic but I shouldn't have been able to see all this coarse grassland and open moors. I should have seen open woodland. Some of the trees had gone because they had been cut down by humans. Most of them had gone via a simple process of allowing sheep or deer to nibble down the young saplings so that given enough time the old trees died out and weren't replaced. Sheep were a highly valuable crop when wool was the main form of clothing. Now that the trees have gone they are still the best way of earning something out of the harsh environment that survives. Only the toughest of plants can cling on out in the open and only the toughest of animals can live off them.

Sheep are clearly tougher than me. A few minutes at the summit in a cold wind were quite enough. Nevertheless, the top of Ingleborough is a stimulating place. Everyone who gets there appears to enjoy arriving. The people I passed all seemed to think it was only right and proper that we should exchange a couple of words. Partly no doubt out of common courtesy. Mainly though out of a mutual recognition that we had all chosen to achieve the same thing and had a right to feel pleased with ourselves and to feel solidarity with anyone else who had matched us. We had worked hard to get here and even though it was cold and looked like it might rain later we had got to the top of the world, or at least as near to the top of it as you can get in Yorkshire. The magnificent views were only a small part of the reward. The main thing was knowing that you had made it. Now I had done so I felt the distinct need to head back to a bit of civilisation and a nice warm cafe.

****

The views aren't quite so stunning in the areas around Clapham in London. The Yorkshire version gives you a sense of your own insignificance in the face of the enormity of nature. In London I tend to get much the same sensation but for a very different reason. I am not overwhelmed by the stark beauty of endless miles of open hills, valleys and moorlands. It is struggling through the enormous numbers of other people with the sensation of hundreds of buildings pressing in around me that tends to bring me down to size. For around 10 years I lived in between Wandsworth and Clapham without ever quite getting used to the anonymity. It was a bit of a run-down area at the time and just about inside the price bracket that enabled me to buy a small one bedroom flat. It was even cheap enough to leave me with some money to spend more time than I should have at the local down at heel pubs. One of them was the Alma. I used to go down there with the woman who later became my wife. Tucked in near to the main roundabout coming off Wandsworth Bridge it was not the most salubrious of locations. Years after we left my wife and I saw it featured in one of the Sunday colour supplements. It had apparently been turned into a boutique hotel. We couldn't resist. It seemed like the ideal opportunity to revisit our old stomping grounds and it would be a bit of a laugh to see whether they really could turn our old beaten up boozer into a boutique hotel. It certainly seemed a very incongruous thing to plant in the heart of a not very posh bit of London.

How wrong could we have been. In the 20 years since we had left a lot had changed. Up the road from the Alma there had been a few neglected shops and behind them the river bank was given over to a builder's yard dominated by a giant sand hopper. Back then, in the bit of abandoned land on the other side of the dual carriageway, in the shadow of busy

Wandsworth Bridge, a group of squatters had set up a bedraggled eco village and put up a few signs about saving the area from rapacious developers. As soon as we started to explore the area it quickly became clear which side had won. The area had gentrified at a pace of knots and, to be ruthlessly honest, looked quite a lot better for the experience. The run down shops had morphed into art galleries and up market boutiques. The sand hopper had gone and been replaced by expensive flats. So had the squatters camp. And the couple of miles of the other side of the shoreline was unrecognisable. The whole of the riverbank had been transformed and what looked like twenty storey buildings stood proudly where a deteriorating power station had been before. The sight of huge chimneys decaying in amongst tatty remnants of concrete bunkers had gone. Instead there was at least a mile of posh housing developments displaying for all to see the attractions of owning your own river side view. Each of the homes I was looking at had been provided with their own balcony looking out over the river and the fortunate residents must have paid eye watering amounts for the privilege of sitting of an evening with a nice glass of wine watching the colours change on the water. Turning our old boozer into a designer hotel wasn't an eccentric act. It was entirely in keeping with the new feel of the area. Wandsworth Bridge had come a long way upmarket.

Walking away from the pub towards our old stamping grounds took me firstly to the anonymous housing estate where we used to live. Yet even this has an interesting tale to tell. London has so many layers to it and has experienced so many different slices of history that almost any back street can reveal surprising sequences of change. The street that I lived in was called Bartholomew Close. That was a Huguenot name. So the area had first been settled by people fleeing religious persecution in France. Louis XIV might have been called the Sun King by some but it is unlikely that many Protestants admired his sunny disposition. He was the King who began the abolition of their rights and started the persecution of those who wouldn't convert that ended in mass slaughter. Around half a million Huguenots got out of the country with their lives and their faith intact and a lot of those ended up in London. The city has been welcoming refugees from religious intolerance for a very long time.

It has also had a long tradition of leaving them to fend for themselves in the cheapest parts of the capital. A significant community of the seventeenth century exiles ended up deciding, just as I had, that the area between Clapham and Wandsworth was all they could afford. So they built up a brave little community there and then did what all waves of immigrants seem to do. They worked hard, appreciated the opportunity to live in peace with their neighbours and got on with making sure that they prospered. But the area was still poor enough in 1840 to become the site of the workhouse. At around this time the life expectancy of Londoners was measured for the first time. It came in at 16 for labourers in the poorest part of town. Someone cared enough about that to add a hospital unit to the workhouse. Whilst they were being morally uplifted and taught the virtues of hard work and a strict diet they also got their health looked after. Gradually the hospital grew in significance. By 1868 a large infirmary had been created with the prime aim of looking after people with TB and that initial building was then extended, changed, messed with, altered, and added to until by the 1970s it was a confusing jumble. These days hospitals are usually shaped like boxes and are designed to have long straight corridors so that patients can be wheeled about easily. The ergonomic designers and cost efficiency teams didn't think much to what was left of St John's hospital. History had left them with a set of imposing buildings that were a very awkward shape indeed. A few turrets and an extra staircase or two looked fine enough but it wasn't quite what was wanted for the modern health service. So they sold off the building and much of the land was transformed into modern flats during a determined drive by the local council to redevelop the area.

The council's initial intention was to build some decent high-quality council homes. Then times and politics changed. It was decided that these new homes were far too nice to be provided on cheap rents for the poor. They were sold off as soon as they were built. I bought mine from someone who had received a nice little subsidy to help her to buy one of them from the council. Which she then proceeded to sell on to me at a good profit.

London is made up of a hugely interesting variety of little neighbourhoods each of which is likely to have a past every bit as complex as this. Even the most anonymous suburb has history. As soon as something looks like it has become a permanent fixture of the landscape times change, and before you know it a different reality has popped up and taken physical shape around you. Walking down towards Clapham Junction I found myself constantly confronted with the contrast between what I had known and what exists now. In the wilds of the Yorkshire moors land can be left virtually unused for decades and no one feels the need to alter its use. In any part of London that is remotely fashionable every inch of land is valued and something is done with it if there is a sniff of a suggestion that the old use might be becoming a bit tired and predictable. Every week a new restaurant is opening. Everywhere properties are being smartened up and rents increased. Look around and someone has come up with a good new idea for how to tempt you to part with your money and enjoy doing it. The opportunities for consumption are relentless but also very attractive. Sometimes a touch too attractive. Especially if all those lovely goods are sitting there tempting you and you haven't got much money because it has all gone on the skyrocketing rents. In 2011 something snapped. Instead of happily browsing the shops and deciding what to buy there was a sudden outpouring of anger and excitement. Riots broke out.

Across the world the riot has often been an important part of popular protest and has been used by the poor and powerless to make a clear political point. They broke out in the United States after Martin Luther King was assassinated. No one had to look very hard for the cause or to think for terribly long before coming up with an explanation of the kinds of things the rioters were seeking to achieve. The effectiveness and the morality of the method was questioned by many but almost everyone could quickly work out what had happened and why without needing to consult a professional sociologist. Much the same was true when riots broke out in Soweto on numerous occasions during the era of apartheid or indeed when the people of Southall and Brixton took to the streets during an earlier phase of London riots in 1981. The violence and the damage to property were widely condemned as doing more harm to the local community than any good that could possibly be done by the publicity gained for political grievances. Those grievances were, nevertheless, pretty clear and most participants could articulate them.

The riots at Clapham Junction in 2011 were rather different. The initial trigger was the death of a black man in a police raid that a lot of people in Tottenham thought of as a deliberate and provocative execution. By the time the word on the street about these events arrived in Clapham there didn't appear to be an awful lot of politics or protest left in what was happening. The raw excitement of participating took off and it seemed as if that had become the sole point. Clapham didn't get a riot with a political purpose. It got riots as a shopping experience. Riots as a fun night out. For some. Hundreds of shops got broken into and people rushed out with everything from mobile phones to bottles of spirits. These weren't riots rejecting the excesses of a consumerist society and trying to breakdown the capitalist system. These were riots by keen and enthusiastic consumers who spotted a good chance to pick up a bit of gear.

For those who actually owned any of the looted shops or worked in them then it wasn't such a nice experience. Standing at the front of a restaurant you have worked your socks off to build up and trying to persuade a group of drunk rioters that they don't want to break it up in order to get at your wine cellar takes courage. Even when someone was prepared to take the risk of trying to do this it didn't always work. Elderly residents who had lived in the area for years cowered in their homes whilst people ran past battering on doors, smashing the odd window and giggling. Then the mood of the crowd got more ugly and attention turned to the biggest and most famous Department Store in the area.

For generations Clapham Junction folk had regarded Arding and Hobbes as one of the most secure and stable features of the very centre of their town. A solid old fashioned Department Store where you could get a kettle, buy your jeans, sip a cup of coffee and order a package holiday. It celebrated its eccentric slightly old fashioned approach even in its architecture. As soon as you came out of Clapham Junction station your eye was almost immediately drawn to the store by a huge dome plonked on the roof line standing proudly above the front entrance and trying to convince you that this really was a very superior store. The shop got badly trashed during the riots and the pictures on the national news showed chaos taking place around its impressive frontage. People were running out of the front of the store carrying flat screen TVs home so that they could watch themselves rioting. A little way up the street others were bravely going into a burning building. In the hope that there was something useful left to steal. As in most riots no one ever found out who had set fire to the building. Nor did most of the really unpleasant participants get caught. A few of those who were late in the day and not in a big enough gang, or who were incompetently struggling home with goods that were too heavy to carry easily, got themselves arrested. The courts gave many of them hard time to discourage the others. Well before they reached the courts and their families worried themselves sick over the consequences of their night of stupidity the whole thing had died down. The storm came quickly and unexpectedly and went pretty much the same way.

Now as I walked past the store I was hard pressed to spot that anything had ever happened. The only real sign was that it had been taken over and renamed. Instead of the area developing a bad reputation and becoming run down the opposite seems to have happened. Clapham has continued to gentrify. In the main shopping street Jamie Oliver has opened an up market kitchen shop and it is doing a roaring trade. Further on, as you enter the local market the change is even more dramatic. When I used to go down to Clapham market to buy my groceries it mainly featured good solid fruit and veg stalls and the most exotic thing you could buy was the fascinating variety of vegetables on the stalls serving mainly the local West Indian community. There was stall after stall of rather sad clothing that looked seriously out of date and a series of frumpy women rummaging through the items in the hope that they could find a floral dress or a sensible pair of knickers that was a little bit cheaper than the other remaindered stock.

Not any longer. The stalls now consisted of artisan bread producers, street snacks produced by gourmet chefs at gourmet prices, regional cheese purveyors and umpteen providers of nice little relishes. There was more chance of finding a designer hand-made beeswax candle in a range of naturally dyed shades than there was of picking up a pair of cheap socks. You could still get some interesting varieties of fruit and veg straight from the West Indies but a lot more of the customers were serious food lovers out researching their latest dinner party than local residents getting the supplies in for the family.

This probably all sounds somewhat contemptuous of the change but actually it works very well. A lot more people look happy exploring the market now than I remember from twenty years ago. Because there is more to enjoy about coming to a place with endless varieties of interesting little ways of tempting you to try something a bit different. I quite like deciding whether I want a Portugese takeaway lunch or something from a vat of authentic African home cooked produce. The bread is also a lot better than the sawdust inspired offerings that were all you could get back in the day. The market has done what all good markets do. It has moved with the times. When I went first went round it three decades ago it had already undergone a major transformation. They weren't always selling Yams and three different varieties of mangos to women who learned how to cook in the West Indies. Back in the nineteenth century they were probably selling watercress and boiled bacon. All good markets change rapidly as soon as their customers change and one of the best things about London is the speed with which that happens. There is always something new and interesting on the market stalls and as soon as someone comes up with a good idea you can be pretty sure that someone else is already working on how to top it. As a consequence, Clapham market remains a real pleasure to explore.

The same is true of Clapham as a whole. This is an area that seems to enjoy change and to thrive on it. Clapham common was once a place where the high spot of the entertainment industry was the opportunity to sail a toy boat in a pond. It is still a charming place to do that if you are so inclined. But there are also a lot of other options. The common is used for music festivals. You can see some well-known and very talented bands running through their set list with well-practiced skill. You can also hear some dreadful attempts to break through to stardom by bands with a lot more ambition than ability. You can join the Friends of Clapham Common and help plant fruit trees and keep the whole place looking in tip top shape. Or you can join with the winos and make your contribution in a rather different direction. I saw evidence of the work of all three, even if the bands were represented by scruffy posters. Busy roads of traffic were passing by on all sides of the common hemming me in with the fumes and the noise of the city. Yet in the centre of the park it was still just possible to get a sense of a little bit of space of your own in the middle of the city and of the way it was being used and valued.

I headed for the north side of the park and walked along a sequence of good solid residential buildings that had been providing homeowners with nice views of the common for a couple of centuries. Many of them had been built out of the light coloured London brick which had aged very attractively. There were two huge 7 storey blocks that had been topped off with roofs of steep slates and ornate railings that would have not looked out of place in a French chateau. Almost every house in the row seemed to have a blue plaque celebrating the life of some grand resident from the past. The first one I spotted paid its respects to the composer Grieg and the last one to the novelist Graham Greene. If I had looked harder and a little further I could have found the homes of Samuel Pepys, Benjamin Franklin or William Wilberforce. This part of London had clearly once been a very respectable place to live. Or, perhaps more accurately, a place where you could live a bit of a bohemian lifestyle on the edge of the city.

Back at the end of the eighteenth century the MP William Wilberforce found it to be a very convenient place to enjoy the company of a community of people who were serious about their religion and serious about abolishing the slave trade. He became the leading light of an informal grouping that later became known as the Clapham Sect. The cheap house prices, in what was then a delightful village on the edge of the expanding city, meant that Henry Thornton, one of Wilberforce's fellow campaigners, could afford a thirty-four bedroom house with its own library and reading room. He used all that space to set up a place where guests could drop in and discuss the latest thinking and that openness was typical of the attitudes this group of people wanted to stimulate. William Hague describes it like this:

"The community created by these impressive individuals was probably unique in its atmosphere. Wholly relaxed in each other's company they observed no restrictions in wandering into each others' homes and gardens, discussing any great cause or biblical text that came to mind."[8]

The combination of furious interest in ideas and equally furious commitment to action proved incredibly powerful and it was from this gathering of like-minded individuals in Clapham that much of the energy came that drove the campaign against the slave trade. Like all good campaigns the gains were not limited to the freedom from horrible slavery for people a long way from Clapham. The gain in terms of community spirit and open-minded attitudes was also very beneficial for the local area. These people of thought and action found an expression for their community spirit by worshipping together at the newly built Church of the Holy Trinity. This made it both a focal point for their village life and a really important location in the history of the abolition of the slave trade. I thought it would be a good idea to end my visit at that church, as a kind of homage to the collective efforts of those fine campaigners.

It wasn't a hard place to find. It sits like a giant rectangular slab of brickwork at the edge of the common only yards from the tube station and streets full of busy traffic. It is, however, curiously deserted. Much of Clapham today is still a vibrant place with a real bustle of energy and activity. A high proportion of the people who walked past me on the streets were young and you could hear many different languages

---

[8] W. Hague, William Wilberforce, (Harper 2008), p219

being spoken on the streets. People are out enjoying the freedoms that the Clapham sect fought so hard to win. But the church where that sect worshipped felt utterly abandoned and seriously run down.

Part of the reason for this is the very seriousness of the community that created it. When you insist on their being few architectural distractions to divert you from focusing your attention on communicating with your God you tend to end up building a very austere structure. Intimidating austerity was certainly the predominant impression that it inspired in me. The walls seemed to loom up above me as I approached and I peered through the plain windows to see a remarkably featureless interior. Rows of benches marched across a large hall. It looked like the sole intention of the architect had been to make sure that as many worshipers as possible could be packed inside the very substantial floor area. Decoration had been kept to an absolute minimum and there were no soaring arches or fine domes. Just a functional room and straightforward rectangular spaces. This was a place that had been built in the clear conviction that the main thing a church needed to worry about was how it was going to pack all the customers in not how pretty it looked.

No one was clamouring to be admitted on the day I visited. All the doors were shut and firmly bolted. Round the front of the church a little architectural flourish had crept in. They had built a very fine entrance using good strong classical pillars to put a roof over the heads of those wanting to linger outside the church and exchange radical ideas, a bit of gossip or looks that might indicate the possibility that one more marriage might be in the offing between community members. That convenient shelter from the wind and the rain coming in off the common was clearly still valued. There was a small sign on the door of the deserted church. It said "Please do not sleep here." It had turned into a very convenient spot for homeless people to gain a bit of refuge.

It seemed to me that, like so many places in history, the Holy Trinity Church in Clapham had seen its glory days and then declined. The members of the Clapham sect who worked so hard to ensure that this was a vibrant place to worship would be horrified to see the state that it has now declined into on a quiet day in midweek. Hopefully they would be a lot happier with the progress of many of the attitudes they also worked so hard to progress. A passion for freedom has turned out to be a more lasting and valuable legacy than bricks and mortar.

Richmond

There aren't many slums in Richmond Upon Thames but many years ago I managed to succeed in renting one. A friend had told me that he was moving back in with his wife and asked if I'd like to take over the tenancy of his flat. I foolishly agreed on the basis of his description of the accommodation and an assumption that in such a posh part of London it couldn't be too bad. When I arrived, and saw for the first time the place where I'd be living, I discovered maggots in the kitchen rubbish bin, a brick missing from the wall in the toilet that allowed cold air straight in from the outside and a pervading smell of damp which this additional unplanned ventilation hadn't succeeded in curing. A week later I discovered that the friend had moved back in. Apparently, his wife took against the discovery of his latest infidelity. He seemed to think that some women could be very unreasonable about these things. She seemed to think that the reconciliation hadn't been entirely a success. This added a degree of overcrowding to the general squalor especially when his young daughter came to stay on the rare occasions that he took on his share of the childcare duties.

Despite this bad start the move proved a success. I enjoyed living in Richmond. Most people do. It is a lively riverside town with all the advantages of being part of the capital coupled with a nice sense of being out of the worst of the overpowering crowds. I particularly liked my regular run. It started out going through the town centre and then circled round via the river and Richmond Park before dropping back down to my seedy flat. This meant that I got a decent climb in early in the run when I was feeling lively and an easy downhill stretch at the end when I was considerably more knackered. So I wanted to go back to Richmond to follow that route again. Not that I remotely thought I could still hack the run. But I did think that I might manage to walk that circuit and to refresh my memory about the sites.

As it happened I ended up going round the circuit even more slowly than I expected. I'd had my knees fixed only two weeks before so it was a case of hobbling a few hundred yards and then finding a bench where I could sit and read the paper or a nice cafe where I could grab a coffee. There was no shortage of either. When you come out of Richmond train station you are disgorged straight into the centre of town. This means that, if you so choose, you can get stuck straight into shopping in the wide variety of clothes stores that ensure the high street remains busy and active. Alternatively, you can cross the busy street that leads into the shopping centre, walk up a small alley and within a few yards you are on Richmond Green. Here it is virtually impossible to remember that you are only yards away from all those shoppers. The Green is the kind of open space that everyone likes. The ideal place to walk your dog. A stylish backdrop for your visit to the gloriously over decorated Richmond Theatre. A location where an old man can sit with his book and watch the world go by. Also a place that every jogger in town seems to pass through in order to show off their latest designer sportswear. On a Saturday morning you can watch people throwing Frisbees, or showing off their Yoga poses, or being so very old fashioned as to start a game of football between people of a variety of ages and sexes relying on the cliche of a few jerseys for goalposts and a lot more enthusiasm than skill. On the early Thursday morning when I went it was considerably quieter and the artisan ice cream shop that fronts onto the Green was not doing quite as much business as it normally would. Richmond in Surrey is that kind of place. If you are going to buy your child an ice cream after you've all run around playing football then it is jolly well going to be a designer ice cream.

Walking the length of the Green took me close to the river. At the far end of it I headed down a couple of rather stylish back alleys and found myself next to one of the best situated pubs in London. The White Cross looks like a classic Victorian boozer that has been smartened up to within an inch of its life but which has still managed to retain some of its character. It fronts directly onto the Thames in one of those parts of London where the river is capable of supplying you with the sight of some interesting wildlife living on a gently moving waterway, instead of providing views of a mess of brown sludge brought in on the tide. One of the great things about living in a river city is that you have access to a fantastic variety of pubs that you can spill out of and relax on the river bank with a pint in your hand. Arrive at the White Cross a bit late for lunch on a hot sunny day during the tourist season and you might struggle to enjoy the experience of battling to get a drink. But if you time it right then it is easy enough to get served and you can join a lively crowd of all ages thoroughly enjoying the sights of the river. In those circumstances this is one of the best places in London to relax and enjoy life.

It was a bit early for a drink when I arrived so I gave the nostalgia of a trip to the bar a miss and headed off up the river. The last time I had been here there was a lot of building work going on and they were constructing one of those housing schemes that are carefully designed to match the eccentric variety of building styles you can find on any normal street in the locality. It had worked. You needed to look hard and long at quite a few of the newer buildings to figure out whether they had been put up over a hundred years ago or during my lifetime. In front of the new development a garden terrace had been put in place that stepped slowly down towards the river. People were sitting at different levels of it chatting or just watching the river flow. Others were riding their bikes along the river front, perhaps having hired them from the gloriously named Blazing Saddles cycle shop. It looked like everyone was having a good time. In fact that is the theme that emerged consistently throughout my visit. People in Richmond seemed to be finding life very easy. In an environment like this it was hard not to.

I was tempted to walk further along the river but instead I followed my old running route at a much slower pace and turned off just after Richmond Bridge so that I could start the long climb up the hill in order to get the reward of one of the best views in London. Shortly after I turned away from the river and started to cut upwards I found myself stood in front of a statue that was tucked into a small garden just beside the bridge. One of the great pleasures of exploring in Britain is that you constantly find yourself running into some unlikely connection between the locality you are in and an important event in history. On this occasion the link turned out to be the fantastically named Bernardo O'Higgins. I've always thought that this man had one of the best fun names of any major historical figure. I had fondly imagined that he must have woken up one day as gold old Irish Bernard Higgins and then decided that it would go down a lot better with the ladies if he spiced it up a bit and went rather more Spanish. As it happens the way he got his name was nothing like my imaginings and derived from a much simpler circumstance.

His father was born in Ireland but came from Spanish descent. Those Spaniards who got shipwrecked on the coast of Ireland after the debacle of the armada had little choice but to settle down and build a new future. There were therefore a number of families of mixed heritage in coastal areas that the sailors reached after going all the way around the north of Scotland to escape the British navy, only to be caught in a storm off the West coast of Ireland. Bernardo was also something of an accident. He was an illegitimate child of mixed heritage who was quickly packed off to Chile to be raised by his mother. Fortunately, his father didn't entirely cut him off without a penny and so as a young man it was decided that he should be sent to Richmond to live modestly whilst he got an education. On one level that succeeded very well. He got an education in the ideals of liberty, a set of connections with radical Freemasonry and entry into the social circles of those with a strong interest in the idea of colonial independence. It may not have been quite what his father had intended.

Nor, I suspect, did his father realise when he left him land in Chile in his will that the young man would end up President of the country or rather - to give him full credit - the First President of a country he had spent years fighting to liberate. Those 3 years in Richmond had inculcated the young man with such a strong commitment to the national independence movement that he gave up the opportunity to live quietly and well on a nice piece of inherited land and instead went for years of hard military campaigns and a well deserved place in history. It might have been a touch more deserved if he had been a bit better at working with others and bit less convinced that his wise and supreme leadership shouldn't be challenged - but extremists that change things are not known for their natural humility and their willingness to compromise. He now has a lot of statues to him in Chile and one rather forlorn one in a corner of a small public gardens right next to Richmond bridge.

I left his statue to its undeserved obscurity and worked my way up Richmond Hill. It is a steep rise past a succession of high end antique shops, art galleries and rather fine cafes interspersed with the homes of people who have serious amounts of money. Georgian frontages with beautiful wrought iron railings seem to be the norm. The higher you climb up the hill the more the houses begin to replace shops and the larger and more expensive they get. I went past an enormous courtyard of very superior Victorian apartments where I could have moved into a small 2 bedroom flat if I had a small fortune to spare and another one available to cover the service charges. Right at the top of the climb the stylish Richmond Hill Hotel occupies pride of place. And a very proud place indeed it is. The summit of the climb is within yards of the magnificent Richmond Park and overlooks one of the most shapely curves of the Thames. Well healed local residents are in the ideal location to live with spectacular views and wonderful surroundings and then stroll down to the tube station and get the District Line into the city and any business meeting or cultural attraction that they might fancy.

The hotel sits on the left of the road where there is a concentration of some of the most stately buildings on Richmond Hill. The right is mainly given over to some lovely public gardens. Up high amongst those gardens I began to get glimpses through the trees of views that made it very clear indeed why this is such a desirable place to live. If you can find a spare seat on the right bench around here, then you can look out across the sweep of the Thames and see the heavily wooded countryside stretching out for mile after mile below you. London suburbs don't immediately strike you as the most likely place to find a woodland but as soon as you gain any height and look out over them you quickly realise just how wooded many of them really are. From up here on Richmond Hill the river seems to disappear into the distance across a huge plain covered with trees between which a few buildings peek out. The view must cover a good fifty miles of countryside and it looks more like a forest than some of the most prime residential land in the country. In fact we have reached the stage with much of British agriculture that if you looked out over fifty miles of prime southern English farmland that you are most likely to be looking at great stretches of uninteresting fields each of which consists of the same crop growing for up to a mile. Few hedgerows and even fewer trees would be permitted to get in the way of agricultural machinery, chemical sprayers and high crop yields on the majority of modern farms. Here, by comparison, there are massive numbers of trees in suburban gardens and parks, along with plenty of hedgerows and trees in smaller fields. Foliage dominates the signs of urban development when you look at the scene from this height and distance. As a consequence, you get the feeling that you are looking upon a landscape that is not that dissimilar to the original primeval forest - provided of course that you are prepared to ignore the sight of a few landmark buildings sticking out from amongst the trees and the noise of the planes passing over your head every two minutes on their way to Heathrow. The most obvious of the large buildings is the Twickenham rugby ground and on a match day you can stand on this hill and just about make out the sound of the crowd getting excited provided that not too many cars pass by and the flight-path isn't proving too noisy.

The sense of being out in the country, despite being in the middle of one of the most crowded urban environments in Europe, was even stronger when I tore myself away from the panoramic view and made my way through the entrance into Richmond Park. There can't be many cities in the world that boast as many parks as London but none of them are remotely on the same scale as Richmond Park. It isn't so much a park as a giant deer estate and wildlife sanctuary that has been fiercely protected by generations of determined town planners and local residents. In the days when I used to live here I thought I was pretty fit and so after running up the hill I would usually take the opportunity to go a bit further and run around different parts of the park exploring. I never managed to cover the whole area. The perimeter road is 12 kilometres in length and I kept on finding new nooks and crannies that I hadn't come across before. Doing so also revealed an impressive array of wildlife that seemed to have decided that London suburbs provided a bit of extra warmth, a lot of extra food and this nice safe habitat where they could hunker down for the night. The park is famous for its deer which are hard to miss and don't take kindly to being disturbed by runners suddenly appearing from unexpected directions. It also has green woodpeckers, the usual London foxes, the occasional heron, kestrels, owls, bats and of course lots of different beetles. Everywhere has lots of different beetles. On one walk in this park I found some excellent edible mushrooms back in the days when so few people were searching them out that it was reasonable to pick them. Now every other restaurant likes to serve wild mushrooms and picking them in somewhere as well visited as this park is a seriously bad idea. It simply isn't possible to allow the number of foodie enthusiasts that now exist in the capital to each take a few and hope that they'll continue to thrive in the park. On this visit, despite going in autumn and being in almost the same location where I had come across large numbers of very nice specimens 35 years previously there were now none in evidence.

I decided to sit down and rest my newly repaired knees on a bench beside a small muddy pond. I was pleased to see that lots of runners were still making good use of the park. A regular succession of them plodded their way past, each one seeming to have spent more on their designer sportswear than the last. It was, perhaps, not entirely a bad thing that I was no longer able to plod round in my old gym shoes and my baggy shorts. I would clearly have been at something of a sartorial disadvantage. Looking out across the park I could see two different types of deer gathering in good sized herds and relaxing in the late morning sunshine. On a small tree just the other side of the muddy pond from me a bird was quietly perching. Then all of a sudden it dived down onto the ground to pick off an insect that had lost patience and come out searching for something to eat. The bird returned back to its perch looking pleased with itself and tried to look every bit as innocent as it had a few seconds before. It wasn't long before something else fell for the trick and it struck lucky again. I looked up the bird when I got home and it turned out to be a Spotted Fly Catcher. Just a small part of the huge variety of life that prospers in the park.

I sat for a long while in the sunshine soaking up the rays and allowing my knee to recover from walking rather further than the doctor had recommended whilst I waited to see how many tasty morsels the flycatcher would gobble up before its cover was blown. Then a runner got a bit too close to it for comfort and it flew off, so I decided that I too would move on. I found a little gate out of the park and worked my way back down the hill through a series of well-kept suburban streets towards the tube station. One of the streets had a very nice selection of shops and cafes so I stopped and got myself some lunch. A little way further down the hill I turned a corner and I found myself on the road where I used to live.

I looked hard at the flats trying to see any evidence of one of them being seedy enough to have been the home I had occupied for nearly a year. They had become very smart indeed and the local tradesmen seemed to be doing quite a bit of very nice business working to make sure that they were becoming even smarter. There were people fixing roofs, a couple of kitchen fitting vans parked on the, and a veritable army of workmen heading purposefully in and out of people's homes. Despite a couple of decades of enthusiastic home improvements, I eventually recognised the right place. It was a high Victorian building that had been broken up into flats. The very top one, where I had lived had a small ventilation brick high up in the wall. When I had been there it was this brick that had been broken and was completely missing, thus providing the unwelcome extra airway that made every trip to the bathroom in winter something of an ordeal. I was pleased to note that sometime over the past 30 odd years someone had taken the trouble to get some scaffolding up there and replace it properly. In fact, virtually every house in the road looked like it had done up. Richmond had been affluent when I lived there but still contained the odd eccentric corner where it was possible to find a run-down flat. Not any longer. Everything had been gentrified inside an inch of its life. And the effort had been worth it. Richmond was looking very fine indeed, even on one of its busiest and least attractive thoroughfares. The town was doing very well for itself. It wasn't hard to see why all those people were happy to pay so much money to live in this environment.

Of course not everyone that lives in Richmond is rich and happy. Everywhere in the country there are always some people who are experiencing genuine suffering. There are people in Richmond Surrey who are drug addicts, deep in a bleak personal depression, in pain, alone and isolated or experiencing serious mental illness. But if you look at the statistics you will find a lot fewer of people with almost any difficulty that you care to name in Richmond Surrey than anywhere else that I travelled to for this book. When it comes to life expectancy, health, educational achievement, housing conditions, wealth or income this place is one of the highest scoring locations in the UK. You can see and feel that in the streets, on the river and in the parks as you walk about the place. It is hard not to feel uplifted as you stroll through a locality like this. It still comes across as one of the easiest places in London to relax and enjoy yourself and to feel that life really can be very easy - provided that you have enough money.

****

Much as I appreciated the attractions of Richmond Surrey I was still left with the strange feeling that something was missing. I couldn't quite work out what it was until shortly after I arrived in its namesake. In Surrey no one had engaged me in conversation the whole time I was there. In North Yorkshire I found myself deep in unexpected and enjoyable conversation almost as soon as I arrived. I'd gone with my wife and we walked down from the long stay car park along a street of fairly anonymous shops. Then we spotted one that looked like it might be interesting. It called itself a licensed grocery and appeared to be purveying an eccentric mix of dirt cheap items like packets of noodles and top of the range designer produce aimed at the passing tourist. It also had a special offer on wicker hampers. Something that you don't see being advertised by too many shops in Surrey. If you do then you can bet a London suburbs mortgage that it won't be at these prices. So we went in and enquired.

Almost as soon as I spoke the shopkeeper wanted to know all about me. In Surrey the shopkeepers were in a rush to make the next sale. In Richmond North Yorkshire it was clear that there was more of a gap between significant chunks of business. If they were going to shift one of their small store of hampers then it was going to be something of an event and they wanted to know what kind of person was buying it off them. I was asked where my accent was from. When I explained that it was from somewhere between Stoke and South Cheshire it led to an exploration of a point of common experience. The shop owner had been to Keele University on the outskirts of Stoke. This in turn led to a discussion about the peculiarities of local accents. Was it the case, he wanted to know, that people in South Cheshire called each other "Duck" when offering an expression of casual endearment to a complete stranger? We therefore began to discuss the other terms of endearment which had been used on us in different regions. "Pet" in Newcastle. "Love" almost anywhere in the regions. "Chuck" when you are close enough to Liverpool for no one to feel they are living up to a stereotype. It didn't occur to him that there were parts of the country where no one would dream of addressing a stranger so fondly and I didn't feel the need to regale him with a description of the level of indifference which is expected and wanted in Richmond Surrey. Instead we went on to discuss at leisure a few other points of common interest in our lives. He wanted to know about a cheese shop he had heard of in my neighbourhood. I enquired about the nature of his business and why he was stocking products which were aimed at two completely different client groups. It turned out that he made a bit of regular income from selling to the locals, a bit more money but more irregularly from selling to the tourists and the vast bulk of his real income from selling luxury hampers up and down the country to wealthy corporate clients to give as gifts to business associates. Before we'd finished we were old friends, he'd offloaded a surplus hamper at a bargain price and I'd been offered a discount on the rest of my intended purchases. It seemed like a propitious start.

We wandered out onto the main square, which was just the size that a main square should be. Big enough to give you the chance to step back and look at the buildings but not so enormous that the wind caused too many problems. It also contained everything that a town square should do. A museum, a town hall, a covered market, a collection of coaching houses and a bunch of bored teenagers hanging around trying to work out how to chat each other up. It also possessed a collection of buildings not one of which seemed to have been built in the same year to the same design but all of which had been keeping each other company for long enough to look like they very firmly belonged. They'd grown up just outside the castle walls so organically that they now succeeded in hiding away the castle. We struggled to find the entrance. Once we did the original purpose of the town immediately became evident. The whole place was here because the river took a great arch around the bottom of a steep cliff face. That cliff made sure that no one was going to be mad enough to try and attack in that direction and if you built here you could stand on top of your walls and see any trouble coming from a long way off. Even more importantly you could let the locals know that you were a force to be reckoned with from just as far. Everyone for miles around could see the castle plonked robustly on top of this promontory and figure out for themselves that someone who could build this wasn't to be messed with.

These days it all made for virtually the ideal picture book castle. Proper crumbling walls that were still strong enough for you to scramble over. Suitably impressive narrow windows out of which you could fire an arrow or glimpse the river hurrying by far below. A decent keep that could be climbed up solid stone stairs provided that you didn't mind your legs turning wobbly and your lungs aching. Then a view into the far distance across one of the most remote Yorkshire Dales which was impressive enough to leave you feeling that you might after all have a problem with vertigo. It even had a central area of grassy mounds interrupted by odd bits of ruined foundations so that children could be allowed to run off some energy and build up their imaginations. All very picture book.

Or not. In times gone by this was a castle put up for a very nasty reason. The Normans had a lot on in 1071. They didn't build things on this scale out of solid stone without a very direct need. Five years after their successful invasion most places that they needed to defend got a simple earth wall and ditch with a bit of stone on the keep if it was absolutely essential. They called it motte and bailey. Around Richmond they needed something more substantial. The north of England didn't get the idea that it was defeated easily. William decided that there was only one way to make sure that they did. He would wipe out great swathes of the population, destroy their livelihoods and give a very clear message to the rest of the country that genocide was his chosen method of dealing with revolt. Between 1069 and 1070 William set about harrying the north so completely it would never recover the ability to challenge him again. Then he needed a base to make sure that he could remind people that he could and would do it again if anyone was left alive who still thought they had enough strength to challenge him. He needed Richmond Castle so that his troops could pour out of it on their solid war horses and deal with the locals without bothering too much whether they were part of the uprising or not. He also needed those locals to know what a powerful man he was and to be intimidated. Once he had finished murdering the families of his enemies in hot blood he clearly thought it would be a good idea to have a reliable base from which he could securely do it in cold blood any time he chose to.

He chose his site well. The castle was never taken. Before long its occupants and their families began to feel that there might be a little more to life than killing the locals. Maybe they could start getting a bit of enjoyment out of the land they had conquered. So the town's market started up almost immediately the castle was created. All those troops needed feeding and supplying with good ale. As a consequence there is a good legacy of local pubs and an open air Saturday market is still an important feature of the town. The current stallholders were doing good business as we left the castle and came back into the main square. It wasn't a big market. It was, nevertheless, highly eccentric. You could get a wooden sculpture of a duck, some very nice fish, a slice of home-made coffee cake, some local lamb, vegetables that had been flown in from Egypt, a jar or two of pickles, a pork and Yorkshire Ale pie, and a pair of over-sized ladies knickers.

Each time we stopped to look at something the stallholder seemed determined to engage us in conversation that went well beyond the usual sales pitch. By the time we'd bought a few things we were desperate for some lunch. So we walked out of the town square following signs to the tourist information office in the hope that they could advise us on somewhere to eat with a bit of local character. The signs petered out after a couple of turns in the road and we never found official advice. Instead we ended up outside a collection of cafes. One did Indian food that owed more to curry and chips than to Bengal. Another claimed to be a German Cafe. It did sausage and chips. The third said it was Italian.

It was as good as its word. We know this because the waitress did what every other local seemed to enjoy doing. She engaged us in conversation. Had we been in the first flush of youth and wrapped up in the fascination of discovering all the little secrets that there are to know about the person you are dining with then this might have been something of a nuisance. When you have lived with each other for decades you have told your partner almost every tale about yourself you are ever going to and the same is true for them. Having a young girl enliven your dinner by telling you snippets of information about her life and the way the cafe is run becomes considerably more welcome. We quickly learned that her family really was Italian. That her Dad could speak five languages. That her Uncle could play the piano. That she felt inadequate because she could neither speak so many languages nor produce a decent tune on an instrument. We discovered how strongly she loved music. Indeed she loved music so much that she periodically sang along to the background music playing quietly over the cafe's tannoy system. Before telling us that there was nowhere locally where she could enjoy good music and a decent night life because the town was so dead. Instead she preferred the bright lights of Darlington where there was so much more going on.

I decided not to tell her what the residents of Richmond-Upon-Surrey would make of the idea that the ideal place to find interesting night life was in Darlington on a Saturday night. In fact I didn't have much opportunity to get a word in edgeways. After she had almost finished telling us about the interesting details of her life the people on the next table joined in our conversation. They too wanted to know what a young person did for fun in a town best suited to retired folk. Then they wanted to know where my wife and I planned on visiting. And next thing we knew we were involved in another lively interchange in which the best walk around town was explained to us along with a description of the main high points along the route. We didn't need the information centre. The locals were so easy to talk to that the information we needed naturally fell into our laps.

It turned out that the ideal walk began down by the railway station, followed the river beneath the castle walls and headed back up to town over the bridge to the West. Along the way we were to take in the Church, the National School, the folly and, if we could find it, the place where the protestants were burned for the good of their souls. And when we got back to the centre of town we certainly mustn't miss the theatre. It seemed distinctly churlish to consider walking anywhere else.

We headed off down Lombard's Wynd towards the river and quickly discovered that the railway station was indeed every bit as lively as we had been promised. You could get all sorts of things there. It had a designer beer store, an artisan bread shop, a cinema, an art gallery, more varieties of chutney and cheese than one person could possibly get through in a lifetime, a coffee shop and a swimming pool across the road. What it didn't have was any trains. Or tracks. Instead of having easy local access into the lively job market of Leeds or being linked easily to the cities of the north-east Richmond was cut off. This was why the waitress hadn't got much of a nightlife. You couldn't get anywhere else very easily. The rail link had been closed off in the 60s and the locals had been forced to make the very best of a bad job. For young people the crippling cost of insuring and running a car meant that most of them were stuck in a small town feeling that there was nothing much to do and little variety of job opportunities. The loss of its railway had turned Richmond Yorkshire into a lovely town for talkative old folks and a place that too many young people were forced to leave if they wanted to make anything of themselves.

Leaving the retail experience train station behind us we headed back over the bridge and followed the river upstream. We were walking towards the steep cliff face that made the castle so easy to defend. The path went across some open grassland and then along a well kept road besides the river Swale. It was doing what all good rivers really should do. It was rushing past, dividing periodically when it encountered a boulder, tumbling over shelves of rock and forming a series of graceful arks before heading underneath a bridge of solid stone arches. It even had a bit of a waterfall and a couple of dippers acrobatically searching for insects a few feet above the rapids. As we approached it we had the impressive limestone rock towering above us on one side and more gentle countryside running down to the river bank on the opposite shore. Here the rock was sandstone and it had formed itself into layers over the millions of years in which it had been formed. It looked as if the mud had steadily washed over the surface, accumulating a little more depth with each passing year for century after century. Then there had been some sudden climate event such as a distant volcano erupting and there had been a break in activity. Before long things had gone back to normal and the mud had started building up again. The result was slab after slab of rock lying horizontally just above the river bank with clear dividing lines between each layer.

All the way along the river bank a series of small children were enjoying themselves. There was plenty for them to do. They could throw stones into the river without being told off. They could paddle about in left over puddles watching to see what would happen when a rubber boot stamped down on the surface of the water. They could run out to the end of a little concrete jetty that had been built just above the waterfall and watch the power of the water. Anxious parents were trying hard to keep an eye out for trouble whilst cutting them enough slack to mean that they had some idea of how to handle a manageable amount of risk. We walked past grateful that we weren't slowed up by similar childcare responsibilities and could set a decent pace. Before long we'd circled the base of the castle following a great sweep of the river and got ourselves over to the far side of the town.

Here there was plenty for us to explore. We walked up to Culloden Tower to see what the aristocracy could do with more money than sense in 1746. You built yourself your very own ruin at the top of a hill and named it after a horrible massacre of the Scots. Then you looked a touch surprised when the rest of the population started calling it a Folly. Fortunately two hundred and seventy years was long enough for the cost and most of the implications of the insult to the Scottish nation to have been forgotten. All that was left was a rather nice walk up a hill, an interesting bit of architecture and a good view of Swaledale receding into the distance. After completing our circuit of the Folly we headed uphill through the outskirts of town.

It was wonderful. Little terraces of aged houses decorated the hill joined together by a series of Wynds that found ever more eccentric ways of connecting through to the one above. Everywhere you went there was a route that looked tempting to walk and the difficulty was deciding which would prove more interesting. We resisted the trails leading back to the castle and kept working our way upwards. Eventually we reached a much wider road called Newbiggin where the buildings were grand enough to require enough distance between the two sides of the road for a coach to turn around comfortably. Horses don't do three point turns when they are pulling a grand carriage. The road had been there long enough for Protestants to have been living around the street in the 1500s during the reign of good Queen Mary. Or at least they had been living there until she decided that some of them should stop living. Just across the road from the site of today's Catholic Church the local Catholics had followed Mary's guidance on how best to deal with freedom of religious choice. They burned one of their neighbours alive on this spot.[9] It had the impact on tolerance and mutual understanding that you might expect. A dedicated protestant called John Foxe decided that it would be a good idea to publish a book listing all the martyrs he could find along with gruesome illustrations of how the deed was done. This grisly work provided him with an

---

[9] Jane Hatcher, The History of Richmond, (Blackthorn Press, 2004) p76

early best seller and lots of people with good excuse to go out and burn a few Catholics in return once Mary died and Protestantism came back into favour. It only took the best part of another hundred years and a civil war for the country to figure out that it makes a lot more sense to let other people decide for themselves what religion, if any, they wish to follow. Let us hope the countries where the Taliban and ISIS have repeated our old mistakes figure that out a bit more rapidly than we did.

Fortunately, the locals didn't spend all their time tormenting each other for their religious beliefs. They also liked a good laugh. The evidence of that is also still there to be found. A good solid building proudly proclaims itself to be the home of the Richmond Operatic Society. But one converted Baptist Church providing raucous entertainment hasn't been enough to satisfy the local appetite for a bit of fun. The real treasure of the town is its Georgian Theatre. It was built in 1788 and is the only place in the country where you can see plays presented in a totally authentic building from the era. Admittedly they closed the place for over a hundred years in 1848 but you can't keep a good business down. In 1963 it was re-opened and is now staging plays again. We finished our trip to Richmond Yorkshire by following the guided tour around it.

As a climax to the visit we couldn't have picked a better place. This was clearly a theatre where the actors needed to be very good at handling an audience. The public were crowded in inches from the players. Directly in front of the performers there is a sunken pit where those with very little money could stare up at you and let you know very quickly if they weren't having fun. Behind them there are a couple of tiers of more expensive seats where a bit of privacy could be bought if you were more interested in getting to know your date than watching the play. Either side of the stage the audience is high up, staring down at you. Somehow, even with today's regulations, they manage to pack 214 people in to a tiny space. The actors have to face them whilst battling with a steep downwards slope that threatens to tip them off the stage to join the audience. The idea was that the audience could easily see right to the back of the stage. The practical impact was an even harder struggle against the odds for anyone bold enough to try and hold their attention. Here you faced your public expecting to encounter a constant hum of background noise, serious heckling and people who were quite prepared to throw things at you if they didn't like the entertainment. This wasn't going a location where a high level of subtlety and sophistication was needed. If you were going to survive here then you were going to have to get your jokes in early and often and make sure you got to the love interest and the violence before anyone had a chance to get bored. If this was what it was like over a hundred years after Shakespeare's day then no wonder there are few words wasted in his writing. I learned more about theatrical technique from one minute standing on that stage than I had from hours of listening to experts talking. The Theatre is a national treasure and makes a visit to Richmond a must for anyone with the remotest interest in performance art.

In fact the town as a whole came out very well from our visit. It was a pleasure to go round. It was also a pleasure to find ourselves in a place where everyone seemed to want to talk to us and have so many interesting things to say. Just before we left my wife went into a shop and I sat alone in the town square for a few minutes and tried to take in the atmosphere. Alongside me a group of local teenagers was hanging about. They had been there most of the day. It was a stark reminder. It is all very well visiting an interesting little town and spending a lovely day exploring the sites. It is another thing altogether to spend a young lifetime trapped with the same old sights and sounds every day with little hope of anything interesting happening. Richmond Yorkshire is great. But it has allowed itself to become an old people's town. The youngsters were bored beyond distraction. For them all this heritage was normality. And, though I liked the place enormously, this group of young people were finding it a very boring normality indeed.

Newtown

There is a town in Russia called Novgorod. It is one of the greatest cultural centres of the whole country having been a place of religious celebration for over 1,000 years. I went there shortly after the collapse of the Soviet Union and saw wall paintings hundreds of years old crumbling away along with the damp plaster. The authorities had made major efforts to preserve parts of their heritage. Inside the massive ancient citadel there were neatly whitewashed walls and astonishingly beautiful gold domed churches that were protected by its staunch medieval walls. But they had not bothered to do anything to save the interiors the churches just outside the battlements. There were too many of them and they had been of too low priority to the Communist government. You could smell the damp and the indifference. Strangely all this neglect added to the atmosphere and enhanced the attraction. I felt like I was in direct contact with the past and exploring it just before it disappeared for ever. The whole place was magical. It had authentic age and a peculiar mixture of perfect preservation of a proud history along with ample evidence of decline into ruin of other parts that same heritage. It was everything that I think of when I imagine a town of great age and authentic beauty. The English translation of Novgorod is simple. It means New Town.

It is not a very good idea to call a place New Town. For a start it shows a certain lack of imagination. There are 29 places carrying the label listed in my atlas of the UK. If you add place names ending in newton to the list you get a whole lot more. It is not exactly a name that marks you out from the crowd. Then there is the small issue that a place tends to get stuck with a name. Long after it has ceased to be appropriate. My local pub is called the New Inn. It was built sometime around 1650. Places that were once a novelty become normality and then age. They need something more than newness in the name that identifies them.

Nevertheless there is something interesting about towns that have sprung up quickly as a result of someone's plan. There are always quirky aspects to them which make them well worth exploring and often they are bold experiments in fresh ways of living which repay the visitor handsomely for spending a bit of time there. Birmingham has Bournville. Mersyside has Port Sunlight. Bradford has Saltaire. And there were a whole series of attempts made by late 60s urban planners to create successful new communities. Some of which went very badly wrong and some of which have prospered. But my favourite example of a new town planned by one courageous visionary has to be Robert Owen's creation of New Lanark. Since Owen was born in a place called Newtown I thought I would cheat a little on my original objective and instead of visiting two places linked solely by a name I would go to the Newtown where he was born and then to the new town he created.

The Newtown of his birth is in Wales. I got there on a Friday in the middle of summer on a fine day. Not much seemed to be happening. I dreaded to think what it would have been like in the middle of winter with the wind driving the rain across deserted streets. It is not a big place. The population just creeps above 10,000 and it is a long journey on slow roads to get anywhere much bigger. I had expected to spend most of my day looking up all the key sites associated with Robert Owen and walking between them. It didn't take me long. There was a very nice museum with some very friendly staff. But it only consisted of a couple of rooms and even with my lifelong interest in the man I struggled to make my visit there last an hour. Finding Robert Owen's birthplace was equally quick and easy. It was above a bank just across the road from the museum. His grave was 100 yards away down a backstreet in the very well-kept grounds of a disused church close to the banks of the river. It has some very fine wrought iron work and a nice dedication from his family. Nearby there was a riverside walk which made for a pleasant but short stroll. I turned back towards town to find the Robert Owen statue put up by the locals. That was another 100 yards away. I had completed my tour of the Robert Owen sites of Newtown in double quick time. So I got in the car and went off to try and work out why the place was consciously created 800 odd years ago.

It turned out that back in the thirteenth century the valley that Newtown sits in was a much more important location than it appears to be now. Indeed it was at the centre of a major conflict that made a huge difference to the history of both Wales and England. The reason was pretty clear to see. The River Severn ambles through the town making graceful curves and running over gentle declines. Alongside the river there is a small floodplain. If you were English and wanted to bring troops into the heart of Wales this made for an ideal route. Nowhere is Wales thinner than around this part of the country. Above the valley there are hills rising above you that are hard to cross and easy to protect. But, if you stuck to the river valley and followed it upstream, you could quickly penetrate deep into the heart of enemy country. Then you could deliver whatever punishment you deemed necessary to the troublesome locals who seemed so unappreciative of the opportunity to pay your taxes. If you were a Welsh king called Llywelyn ap Gruffudd then it made an equally tempting route out of the country to attack.

So the English, following the instructions of Henry III, built a castle on the edge of the entry to this area with every intention of making it clear who had the strongest army and the most resources to draw on. It sits on an intimidating hill just above Montgommery. In response Llywelyn squeezed every tax he could raise from across the parts of Wales he controlled and used a great deal of the money to build a castle on an equally intimidating hill at Dolforwyn. This one dominates the Severn Valley just a couple of miles downstream from Newtown. I found the climb up to each of the castles a hard slog even for a tourist with sturdy shoes following a convenient well signed path. If you were thinking about fighting your way up these slopes and then tackling these good strong walls under enemy fire you would be very sensible to think again.

At first both sides looked hard at the defences of the other lot and decided to make the best of a bad thing and keep to a peace treaty. It held reasonably well. Then Llywelyn got married. Which might have been fine if he had gone for a good Welsh girl that was no threat to the English. Instead he went for Eleanor de Montfort which gave him connections that were rather too fancy for the liking of recently crowned Edward I. Having a potential enemy with a powerful new wife and a powerful new castle so close to his border and some of his most productive land was not something Edward felt happy about. He decided that the time had come to show Llywelyn how much more powerful your army is when you have a customs revenue of £10,000 a year at your disposal and your Welsh opponent has only £17[10]. As is the way with these things he didn't just invade. He contrived to make sure that a couple of the usual border incidents got blown up into a serious dispute and then he had a good excuse to dispatch as many troops as he could to settle the issue in earnest.

The nice new Welsh castle proved less useful than it looked. It was in a really difficult location to attack and seemed very intimidating but, astonishingly for Wales, it didn't have a reliable water supply. Consequently, it didn't hold out long. With aggressive well-armed troops opening up a route that allowed him to get deep into Wales, Edward soon got the better of the battles. Llywelyn was utterly defeated. With consequences for the subjugation of what became a mere Principality that aren't popular with a lot of people to this day.

The castle without a decent well got given to a loyal subject of Edward I, called Roger Mortimer, who could be relied on both

---

[10] Marc Morris, Edward 1st, A Great and Terrible King (Hutchinson 2008), p136

to start digging a little deeper for his water and to keep the Welsh under control. But once the new owners began to feel more secure it was not long before they realised that sitting on top of a steep hill was fine, if all you needed was a great location for defence, but it was a terrible place for anyone associated with the castle to do much profitable trade. So they established a new town down near a convenient crossing point on the river where people would find it easy to come and trade their goods. It worked and the new town began to prosper. Like Novgorod this Newtown has therefore been there a very long time. The charter for the market was first granted in 1279.

The market is still there and it has some interesting little stalls in a nice warm hall in the centre of town. But it is not a big market and after spending my afternoon walking around town I was still left with the over-riding impression that not much happens in Newtown. It has a light and airy art gallery, a lively community centre and some remarkably friendly people but it wasn't immediately obvious where you were going to find a wild time on a Friday night. So I settled down outside a pub with an excellent pint and watched to see what the locals would get up to. It quickly became evident that they were a determined lot. Determined that they were going to have a good time on a Friday night regardless of how small and quiet their town was. Opposite the pub where I was sitting was a small cash and carry stall. A car drove up containing a very large group of people in their early twenties. One of them somehow managed to climb out over the other bodies and staggered into the shop. A few minutes later she emerged carrying enormous quantities of alcohol which was dragged into the heart of the car along with her. They drove off singing at the top of their lungs a somewhat ragged accompaniment to a very loud sound system. I didn't know where they were going but I was pretty confident that they were in for a good time. Then another car pulled up. It contained a family of West Indian origin. Rarely have I seen a better turned out or more dapper collection of people. It reminded me of Brixton in the 1970s when there were a lot of black people who couldn't afford decent accommodation but could afford to dress well and took a lot of pride in doing so. This group of Newtown residents also loaded up with alcohol but they were a lot more dignified and stylish about it. It began to feel like the entire town was busy making equally careful arrangements to enjoy themselves. It wasn't obvious to an outsider where the action was but it seemed more than obvious to the locals that they were going to have to create it themselves. As the night wore on and more alcohol was consumed it quickly became evident that they were very talented at doing so. A lot of people seemed to be having a lot of fun.

****

It is possible that the town was just as lively on a Friday night in 1771. What is certain is that in that year when the most famous son of the town, Robert Owen, was born there Newtown was an equally long way from the mainstream of economic activity. Being born in something of a backwater to a Sadler for a father does not have all the marks of a fortunate start to life. Being a sixth child of seven couldn't have helped either. At first it didn't seem to get much better. Owen was 10 when his father sent him away to work as a draper in Stanford in Lincolnshire.

But this ten year old boy, starting his working life a long way from home and family, was not the type to let it hold him back. Before another 10 years had passed he had borrowed the then huge sum of £100 to start up a business as a manufacturer of spinning mules and made enough of a success of it to attract attention and win respect. His work and his ability to charm were so impressive that at the age of 21 he was offered the job of manager of a textile factory in Manchester. There were negative mutterings. Even then putting a raw 21 year old in charge of a significant business enterprise was a long way from the norm. He did well. He made money for the owner and he made money for himself. He also made contacts.

One of them was David Dale who was the leading partner in a large cotton spinning factory in Lanarkshire. Owen got on well with him. So well that he married his daughter and in 1799 at the age of 28 he bought the factory off his new father in law. He organised it along exceptionally efficient lines. Using the latest modern machinery he carefully thought through the work flow from beginning to end – driving down costs and implementing a rigorous division of labour which made the factory workers exceptionally productive. Little time was wasted waiting for materials to be delivered or transported to the next stage of the productive process. Each person focused on one small part of the manufacture with tools and the materials close to hand, becoming highly skilled at that one job but requiring a minimum of training in order to tackle that task or to move on to a new one. As a consequence the factory produced consistent high quality yarn at great speed and at very low cost. The profits came in equally rapidly.

So far so impressive. Small town boy makes good by his own efforts, marries a wealthy daughter and makes more money than he could ever have dreamed of. This has now become something of a cliché. At the time it was something spectacularly new. This achievement was right at the start of the creation of a capitalist system, at a time when most people knew their place and kept to it. Self-made men were a fresh and exotic breed (and self-made women didn't get much of a look in). Technology was very much in its infancy. This was before the steam engine had been efficiently adapted to drive textile machinery and the factory had to be sited on an obscure out of the way river valley to run off water power. Owen was therefore not just copying the idea of the production line and applying a few new concepts - as later pioneers like Henry Ford were able to do. He was part of the process of inventing the whole idea of large scale factory production and as such deserves to be well known to history just for his ideas on how to organise work. He figured out from first principles how to produce goods efficiently and how to take a small amount of money and turn it into a moderate amount and then to take that moderate amount and transform it into a fortune.

But Owen wasn't satisfied with playing a successful part in the invention of the factory and getting rich quick in the process. He thought about what he was doing and the consequences of it for others. There were plenty of people at the time who were content to make a lot of money and not worry too much if doing so produced suffering for others. Owen was different. He didn't just want to run a factory and turn a profit. He wanted to see if it could be done to the benefit of everyone who worked in that factory rather than just the owner. He wanted to see if it could be accompanied by decent living conditions, proper education and training, a rich social life and clean honest food on sale in the shops. And gradually his ambition grew into a desire to create a completely new society. Starting by creating a whole new town around his factory in Lanarkshire.

We are well used now to the concept of the entrepreneur who makes a lot of money and then turns philanthropist. Owen was the first to do it on any scale. Titus Salt in Bradford created Salts Mill in 1853. Owen was over 50 years ahead of him. The Cadburys started their plans for Bournville in the 1860s. Owen was over 60 years in advance of them. Port Sunlight was created by the Lever brothers in 1888. Owen beat them by 90 years or so.

What he did shocked and excited his contemporaries. It is not difficult to see why. In 1789 the French revolution had made people very aware of how vulnerable a country could be to an uprising of the people. It was also very clear that something fundamental was changing in the economy and in social relationships. The beginnings of factories and of industrial cities were creating places of work that looked horrific and potentially politically dangerous. Well-off people who had been brought up in a largely agricultural community under the assumption that most work is conducted out of doors were shocked rigid by seeing the conditions that existed in many of the first factories and the crowded stinking slums that surrounded them. It was clear at the time that the number and the size of the factories and the industrial towns was growing very rapidly. It was also very clear that the people working in them didn't have an awful lot of reasons to be loyal subjects of a ruling class that had inherited their wealth and power. The combination of a revolution on your doorstep at the same time as a social revolution in your back yard gave pause for thought to many.

So when Owen came forward with a practical demonstration that it didn't have to be like this and that factories could be run by humane methods and produce happy and contented workers whilst also turning a very nice profit he found a very interested audience. The rich and the powerful came in their droves to visit his new town and to see the future. Two centuries later they are still coming. It is now a world heritage site. One of the first things that strikes the visitor is the size of the development. I had arrived expecting to see a small factory and a few houses along with a schoolroom and a couple of other buildings. Instead the scale is truly epic.

The factory, or rather the various different factories, loom up next to the fast flowing river that powered them. Row after row of windows stretch for what looks like a good hundred yards across several storeys in the main building. Close by are a collection of neat homes built to house the workers. It wasn't uncommon for factory owners to need to build homes for their workers if their factories were in remote valleys where they needed to locate to get sufficient water power. It was uncommon for them to be built to the standards of these homes. It was also fairly common for factory owners to build a shop for their workers to use. Owen did exactly that but instead of supplying dodgy cheaply produced foodstuffs at exorbitant prices Owen's shop worked very differently. All the produce was of the highest standards and it was sold at very reasonable prices. What happened to the profits from the sales was even more remarkable. He used that, along with quite a bit of the income from the factory, to finance a school for the children of the workers. Instead of expecting the children to crawl under machines he taught them science, geography and country dancing. At the weekends and in the evening the adults at the factory got to put their own dancing skills to the test in the social club that he established for them. They also got an opportunity to listen to uplifting lectures on subjects of interest such as natural history and access to a library of good quality reading material. Not perhaps quite the equal of virtual reality video games but very fine entertainment by the standards of the day.

Then the factory got hit by one of the periodic recessions which seemed to be an integral part and parcel of the industrial economy that was emerging. Sales slowed up and the workers started to worry that they were about to be thrown out of work. Owen looked at the profits he had made during the good times and came to the conclusion that he could weather the storm. He offered them fewer hours and extra adult education instead of redundancy . He also started to bring the workers into making decisions about the running of the community. All this meant that the succession of important people that he showed round his idea of a New Town came away very impressed indeed. Everyone liked the idea of Owen being generous with his profits and making sure his workers were loyal instead of resentful and rebellious. They were often particularly impressed by meeting his well spoken, well educated workers - something that most of them thought was simply not possible for the brutish working classes.

But Owen eventually made one big mistake. He tried to get those with power and influence to adopt his ideas. He appeared before a committee of MP's and attempted to persuade them that they should ban the practice of children working in factories and establish universal free education. The MPs and the experts listened respectfully to the good Mr Owen. Then they listened even more respectfully to the other factory owners who told them that this was unrealistic pie in the sky, they couldn't afford to do it, and it was a bad idea to educate too many of the working classes in case they got ideas above their station. Owen lost.

Suddenly he started to move from being the darling of polite society and an example to all and instead began to be cast as a dangerous troublemaker. Which is exactly what he proceeded to become. He ceased to be content to be the founder of a new town. He wanted to be the founder of a new society. So he extended the principles that he had successfully applied in practice in one town and decided that they could work for an entire country. He proposed that the way to deal with the recession that was troubling the country was for the government to spend money on public works to put the economy back in action. An idea that Keynes thought he had invented in the 1930s and which produced the 30 years of increased prosperity that followed the Second World War. When that pioneering idea of Owen's was ignored and rejected he proposed a network of co-operative shops across the country supplying cheap and reliable food and sharing the profits. A couple of decades later the idea got taken up in Rochdale and proved a huge success - eventually spreading to a worldwide Co-operative movement that has helped millions. Since at the time the idea was proving slow to catch on and his government seemed determined to reject even the mildest proposals for social improvement Owen decided to bypass governments and establish a network of towns and communities run by their inhabitants. When he couldn't get the land to do this on a large enough scale in Britain he left the country and New Lanark and went off to try and build an even bigger example of a successful community out in the States. He established a large new town in a place called New Harmony. Here everything was to be organised on co-operative principles.

Overreaching himself, and unable to work out how to give the community control but also exercise a degree of leadership, he lost a lot of money and credibility on the failure of most of the American community's ventures. Enough survived to provide some fertile ground for his son to build on but he left the States disappointed by the experience. He came back to Britain with just enough resources to survive tolerably comfortably, sold his share of New Lanark, and spent his time campaigning for women's rights, easy divorce, social justice, co-operative communities, labour notes instead of money, and an end to organised religion. A lot of those messages struck a chord with early socialists and early social reformers. A few did not. Speaking out against religion was the one that caused him the most problems, closely followed by the idea of free love and women having the right to get rid of bad husbands. He ended his life as a somewhat sidelined figure whose book on New Lanark was much read but who wasn't always welcome to put his current views forward in case he said something a bit too radical for his audience.

His ideas are clearly still too radical for many. As you go round New Lanark there are lots of notices pointing out the pioneering work he did on education, housing and shopping. There is a lot less about the challenging thoughts of his later life. What you can find instead is the opportunity to ride in small pods through a part of the factory while you are provided with video projections of actors. They appear on the walls as you pass by and try and explain to you what happened here and why it was so special. A group of very bored school children were being shown onto the train as I boarded it. They clearly didn't share much of my fascination with the subject of new towns. There is a theory that the first flush of adolescence may not be the ideal time in life to absorb factual information about the importance of social reformers. It certainly seemed to be true on this particular morning. These kids looked like they had more interesting things on their minds than the history of factory reform and the emergence of the socialist movement. Video games and the opposite sex for example. They had heard all this boring history stuff before and had better things to do with their time. Almost as soon as they were successfully herded into their pods to journey through the exhibition they fell to enlivening the experience by pushing and pulling each other in innocent fun until the girls descended into a fit of giggles.

I began to feel some sympathy with their indifference. I sat in my little plastic carriage feeling distinctly at odds with the world and wondered what on earth I was doing on this ludicrous indoor train track. Owen's brave attempts to change the world had been turned into a miniature theme park ride where the sights were not dramatic enough to satisfy the short attention span of modern consumers of information.

They say that it is not a great idea to meet your heroes. I began to think that it is not always a great idea to see what they have done to the new town created by one of mine. The gap between the uplifting experience I had aimed for and the desperately banal experience of the themed train ride was a lot more than I had bargained for. I went outside to get some fresh air and almost as soon as I got away from the rather daft attempts to modernise the visitor experience I started to cheer up.

New Lanark remains an impressive place to visit. You can stand in the school room where all those young kids were educated and discover that Owen insisted that this must take place without a single physical punishment and the children must be motivated by a willingness to learn. You can visit his house and see the lists of the famous people who came here and wondered how the raw working class kids could be taught like that when their own kids were subjected to regular beatings at the best public schools. You can see his factory floor and the colour coded display system he used to praise or shame each individual according to how hard they had laboured in the past week. Or you can simply sit on the wall next to the factories and watch the river flow past downstream.

To have started out in such a small backwater and ended up making such a massive contribution to improving the lives of ordinary people makes Owen a very great man. After all this time it remains inspiring to see the power of his imagination turned into physical reality. Provided, of course, that you are not an otherwise occupied adolescent.[11]

---

[11] For this section the prime sources I used were: Robert Owen, The Life of Robert Owen, (London, G Bell, 1920, original 1858); Robert Owen, The Life of Robert Owen, Supplementary Appendix; Robert Owen, New View of Society (1813/14): Robert Owen, Report to the County of Lanark (1821); A.L. Morton, The Life and ideas of Robert Owen, Lawrence and Wishart, London, 1962), Margaret Cole, Robert Owen of New Lanark, (Batchworth Press, London, 1953); J. C. Harrison, Robert Owen and the Owenites in Britain and America,(Routledge and Kegan Paul, 1969); Ian Donnachie, Robert Owen Social Visionary, (Tuckwell Press, Edinburgh, 2000).

Newcastle

If calling a place New Town is a bit of a daft idea then calling it New Castle is every bit as short sighted. Give it long enough and the castle starts to deteriorate and you end up with a place that is defined by an association with the ancient remnants of a building that was once so new and shiny. Two of the UK's large urban centres got stuck with this inappropriate name - Newcastle Upon Tyne and Newcastle Under Lyme. Both of them are old and neither of them has an intact castle. It is the place on the Tyne that most people think of first when they hear the word Newcastle. In my case it is the other way round. I was brought up a little way down the road from the lesser known of these great urban complexes - the one near Stoke that lies in the heart of the Potteries. Newcastle Under Lyme is not the most famous of locations in the country. Nor is it the most prosperous. But it is one of the most interesting. If only because it so clearly demonstrates what happens when times change and industries come and go.

It would be reasonable to expect that this Newcastle would have built its former industrial success in the same way as most of the rest of the Potteries. But it is not particularly a centre for ceramics. It was more of a centre for other trades like textiles. Nevertheless, the town very much shared the same pattern of growth and decline as the wider Potteries - and for very similar reasons. The industries in this part of Britain grew and became internationally successful because of a fierce determination to develop cutting edge technology, a genius for designing new and innovative products that excited the consumer and brilliant marketing initiatives. They declined when the people running them lost sight of all those skills. Too many staff found that they were being managed by people who were more interested in mixing with their existing customers to enjoy a good lunch and a few drinks at the Potters' Club than they were in spotting the next change and setting about making sure that they were at the forefront of creating it.

The early pots manufactured in the area around Stoke on Trent were heavy brown earthenware products that lacked any sophistication. When anyone who had eaten off a crude heavy plate like this first came across a piece of Chinese porcelain it must have been a complete shock to the senses. Lighter, stronger, wonderfully decorated, and a pleasure to touch there wasn't much doubt about which was preferable to own. You only had to hold the two products for a couple of seconds to know which one you wanted. The only problem was that Chinese imports were very costly and way out of the reach of the ordinary person. They couldn't be made locally because no one in the UK understood the techniques that would enable them to make porcelain. That didn't stop the early industrial pioneers in Staffordshire for long. They had the vision, the determination and the self confidence to conduct thousands of hours of experiments in order to figure out how to produce top class porcelain cheaply and easily using Cornish clay fired by Staffordshire coal before glazing it with Cheshire salt.

But they weren't content to stop there and simply imitate Chinese quality and Chinese designs. Wedgewood's genius was to carry on experimenting on colour and glaze and to design pottery that looked fresh and interesting and appealed to the tastes of the middle class. Then he proved an equal genius at getting what he had made into the marketplace via displays in fine London locations and some of the very first 'easy' payment purchase schemes. It was not long before Wedgewood had moved on from selling huge quantities of blue and white imitations of Chinese designs that he cleverly called 'Willow Pattern'. He was soon producing radical and exciting designs of his own. Concepts that no one had ever seen before, such as Jasperware. Products that were so attractive that people who already owned one of his other dinner services were suddenly very keen to buy a second that they didn't really need, but did really want.

As a school child I was taken round the local pot banks and this tale of the clever marriage of science, design, and sales was drummed into me. So fifty years later when my wife and I decided that we needed a new dinner service I thought that it would be a great idea to head off to the Potteries, look around some of the factory shops and get ourselves a bargain direct from the producers. As ideas go it was not a great success. The first two factories we visited had closed recently. There were still plenty of signs pointing us in the right direction but when we reached our destination there were buddleia bushes growing out of the roof of the giant red brick establishments and the car parks were fenced off. An air of desolation and of despair hung around these places and the bustle of people working had been sucked out of these factories leaving an empty shell. We pushed on and eventually found a couple of businesses that were still working and that had functioning factory shops. Walking in to them it quickly became evident why there was so much decline. The porcelain was still of exceptional quality. The designs were not. The first dinner service I looked at had exactly the same pattern as one I had seen fifty years ago as a child. Even then it had seemed old fashioned and unattractive. It had reminded me of the crockery that I had seen on display in my grandmothers' cupboard. Things that were never allowed to be used and that had been kept so long that they had ceased to be in line with the tastes of the 1960s. Decades later seeing the exact same designs on sale seemed like a very strange way to tempt customers to part with their hard earned cash. The offerings looked more like museum pieces than something anyone would genuinely want to buy.

Actually that is unfair. To the museums. Many of the locally made objects in The Stoke on Trent Museum show an astonishing level of vibrancy and sophistication. After a day's fruitless searching in the factory shops of early 21st century we failed to find anything that seemed modern and attractive or remotely matched up to the design standards of the past. The local colleges were still turning out imaginative local pottery artists and you could see their wares on display in the museum, admire their skills and hanker after their products. But not enough of them were being snapped up by local companies ambitious to be at the cutting edge of design. All too often the same old same old was being churned out. So the next week we went to an out of town shopping centre miles from the Potteries where some excellent new designs caught our eye and captured our custom. The crockery we bought was made in the United States.

There is a myth that the Potteries lost its industry because of cheap foreign competition. That may have played its part but it certainly isn't the only reason for the decline. We bought our new dinner service from a part of the world where wages must have been significantly higher than they were in my old home area. What mainly did for the Potteries was not cheap production elsewhere but a failure to keep pushing forward with new design and technology. Too many managers got too comfortable and decided that it was better to keep on doing what the firm had always done and talking to the customers it had always had. The inevitable result was that the companies became set in their ways and their products became uninteresting. When the old customers died off they weren't replaced by new ones and innovative ideas began to come from other locations in the world.

The loss of jobs and industries are not always bad things. Mines are not great places to work down and a lot of factories had dreadful working conditions. But in the Potteries a lot of the jobs were highly skilled and highly desirable and there was no technological change that resulted in people ceasing to want to buy crockery. All that happened was that people stopped wanting to buy the products made in Staffordshire in enough quantities to keep much of the local industry alive because the products weren't designed for the modern market. In many industrial towns the people who lost jobs in the factories were mainly men. In the Potteries a lot of those jobs were done by women and often they were working on very well-paid tasks. Ceramics requires dexterity and an eye for design and it was possible for ordinary working class women to earn excellent livings painting good clear lines onto delicate pre-fired plates as they rotated them on tiny turntables. Others neatly floated transfers off printed sheets and slid them carefully into the exact centre of a seemingly endless line of perfectly shaped soup bowls. Some even worked on drawing fresh new designs or hand painting with great artistic skill the most expensive individually designed masterpieces. Or rather mistress pieces.

Coming home with decent wages in your pocket after a week of highly skilled work put a lot of economic power and sassy attitude into the women of the potteries. As a consequence there has been an admirable tradition of strong women who knew their own mind and knew their own worth for a long time in this area. The loss of those jobs meant not just a loss of income but a loss of a way of life and a loss of a source of pride, identity and financial independence.

This wasn't the case in all sectors of industry. One of the main employers in Newcastle Under Lyme for many years was a huge textile factory called Enderley Mills. The women there didn't always have quite such a good time of it. In the early days conditions in the factory were such that not enough people were prepared to work there and the company was badly short of labour. Enderley Mills decided to solve their problem by going over to Ireland to recruit young girls. It was a point of pride for the company that they looked after them well. After a few years of loyal service the employer found local husbands for the young women. It is not easy to imagine anyone in a pot bank telling their skilled women employees that the company would decide for them who they might wish to marry but in the early days this particular textile factory got away with it for many years.

In the 1960s, when my father worked there as the sales manager, this practice had changed. But the girls were still expected to stand up all day at their sewing machines. Great belts stretching the whole length of the factory drove the machines and giant presses were used to shape and mould fabrics into the forms needed to make military caps and police helmets. Some of those presses and much of the roof of the building that the factory occupied contained asbestos. As a result, a significant number of the women who stood at the machines got the horrible disease mesothelioma which comes from having sharp asbestos particles irritating your lungs and provoking a nasty form of cancer. The relatives of these women brought successful prosecutions for compensation in the 1970s and received substantial damages. The company simply hadn't understood or planned for the dangers until the damage was done and hadn't had the cash or the willpower to deal with them properly once it did.

But the jobs at this factory were crucial to the town. At one stage 1,500 people were employed there on making high quality military clothing. This specialist niche market meant that the jobs lasted much longer than most in the textile industry. The clothing industry was one of the first of the British industries to experience serious loss of jobs to foreign competition. The level of skills and the machinery required are relatively easy to replicate in countries where labour is a lot cheaper than it is in England. So mill after mill closed down in the 1960s and by the early 70s there was almost nothing left. In Newcastle the textile industry clung on longer. Uniform clothing isn't quite as simple to produce as many other clothing items and quality matters to many organisations that require their staff to wear standardised branded clothing. Employers like their staff to be turned out neatly in order to impress their customers and so the technical skills of the Newcastle Under Lyme workers were in demand. This is particularly true of the military and even more true of jumped up dictators. A bit of nice braid and a fine display from your guard of honour is high on the shopping list of men who get to power via a military coup. So it was Enderley Mills that supplied Colonel Gaddafi with the cap that he always wore. Along with several million pounds worth of other military clothing. I know this because as sales manager for the Mills my father sold the uniforms to the Libyans[12]. He also sold specialist military clothing to the Iraqis. This might be thought to be a bit of an extreme and even a traitorous method of keeping a clothing company in business. Actually at the time he sold the clothing it was to help the Iraqis under Saddam Husain to fight a war with the Iranians. The UK happened to be friends with the Iraqis during that war and so the foreign office organised for the company to receive the Queens Award for Industry for their innovative efforts to keep the textile industry alive in the potteries. A few years later the same clothing was pulled out on prime time TV to demonstrate that the Iraqis owned chemical warfare clothing and so must have been planning to use weapons of mass destruction.

The number of unpleasant military regimes who want to show off their elite soldiers in smart new uniforms has not showed much sign of declining. Nor has the demand for high quality military clothing to help soldiers to fight in particular conditions. So the factory in Newcastle wasn't doomed to lose custom and decline. Like the pottery industry, it could have continued, modernised and prospered. Instead what I found when I started walking around Newcastle Under Lyme was a shopping centre and a housing development standing where the factory had once been. The housing developer had been very sensitive to local history as it was demolished. They

---

[12] See his autobiography, Ken Brown, A Stitch in Time, Amazon books, 2017

named the housing estate after the factory. You can get a nice flat in 'The Mill' on Enderley Street very cheaply indeed.

The low house prices reflect what has happened to the community. As a lot of the jobs have gone so has the incentive to move here. There is now more chance of an IT company from Ireland arriving in the potteries to look for new recruits than there is of young women deciding that the only way they can secure their future is to emigrate to Newcastle Under Lyme in order to better themselves and find a high earning husband. There are signs of the decline and the neglect which this community has been left with all over the town. Not that there aren't plenty of very nice buildings in the locality. Or indeed that the town centre lacks character and interest. There are still plenty of fine old buildings in the place and efforts have been made to maintain a consistent skyline and style. The pedestrianised centre is made up of extraordinarily wide streets designed to enable grand carriages to turn around. This meant that I could get plenty of uninterrupted views across a large central square of great stretches of red brick shops. Local history photographs show them as having once neatly framed a vibrant and rather posh shopping centre.[13] There isn't much posh about it now. The Guildhall, right in the centre of the main square, is a fine enough building to be a great advert for the town. Instead it reeks of neglect and sits in the middle of the shopping area looking like an eyesore and an accusation of lack of care. Too many of the shops have become charity outlets and quite a number of the chain stores have tired frontages that look like someone in head office had decided to cut spending here to the bone and dispense with any refits. I also couldn't see a whole lot of customers.

It is possible that this was a result of arriving on a wet cold day in the middle of January. But it was a Saturday morning. The wide expanse of open space that provided the opportunity to

---

[13] Neil Collingwood & Gregor Shufflebottom, Newcastle Under Lyme Through Time, (Amberly, 2012)

look up and see what had once been a very attractive skyline also resulted in the few shoppers that there were being spread very thinly. A cold wind whipped across the square and a touch of drizzle had people pulling their coats tightly around them and hurrying about their business. I felt sorry for the market traders who were stuck out in the cruel wind standing besides very nice arrays of fresh vegetables that had never seen a supermarket shrink wrap. I have rarely seen people look so cold or miserable as they waited patiently for the rare sight of a customer. Looking around the town it proved quite easy to find some interesting and quirky places where people could have spent their money. You would have had no difficulty in buying fishing tackle or getting a tattoo, you could get excellent organic meat from an shop housed in a beautiful black and white building that had been there for centuries, and there were some excellent unspoiled pubs in quirky and interesting buildings. But there were also some horrible soul-less places where the owners had gutted all character out of a fine old building and then done it up very cheaply indeed.

I suspect that the people that would once have shopped here were sitting at home ordering products online in the warmth, or doing their weekly shop in an out of town shopping centre. Newcastle Under Lyme also suffers from the simple fact that it is not the main shopping centre for the Potteries. If you want the best selection of shops you either go to nearby Hanley or you drive down a dual carriageway calling in at the line of superstores. Faced with this barrage of competition the town centre had done well to survive at all. By the time I left the multi-storey carpark had filled up quite a bit and people were starting to turn out of their homes and start shopping. But it was clear that the town centre had been in decline for a long time. Not just because the industry had gone and along with it too much local spending power. Also because, like so many towns, the strength of the main streets had been sucked dry by planners allowing endless constructions of out of town shopping complexes. A place with a proud history that really could have offered an attractive experience was being destroyed by weak planning rules that left the local planners at the mercy of supermarket lawyers. A once high class shopping centre had been heading downhill for a long time.

The anger that comes from decades of neglect and unnecessary decline could be clearly seen when it came to the EU referendum vote in 2016. In Newcastle Under Lyme almost 37% of people voted that they wanted to Remain in the EU. 63% voted that they didn't. That was one of the highest negative votes in the country. Regardless of the way they voted, virtually every commentator put this down to one prime emotion. Local people were angry. They felt they had been let down and neglected. They had spent decades watching the lifestyles that they knew and understood disappear in front of their eyes and they didn't like that and were desperate for something to change.

However bad the conditions may have been at some stages in factories such as Enderley Mills there was also something very positive about working in them. When over a thousand people arrive every day at the same workplace there is a pleasure to be had in talking to friends and neighbours who work alongside you. The work is made considerably easier by the jokes the chats at break time and the feeling that you belong to a community that takes care of its own. These were places where if something bad happened to one of their own it would be minutes before they were organising a whip round and the contributions were generous. They were also places where if the treatment of an individual or of a group was unfair then there were unions that had strong roots in the local community that would stand up for them with a good chance of winning. When it came to the weekend there was enough money around to get by, not at high standards of living, but at standards of living that afforded the odd luxury. People here could afford to buy themselves a nice tea service if they wished to. They could afford to go out on a Friday night and have a couple of drinks. And they could afford to go to the football at the weekend.

If this sounds like a dangerously nostalgic eulogy for a past age in which people died of asbestosis and stood all day working hard long hours then it is at least worth recognising that there are a great number of people who hold hard to the same illusion. It is a lifestyle that a lot of working class people regard as part of their birthright and would dearly like to come back. There aren't many places in the world where the old men and women can tell the youngsters that things were better in times gone by and get believed quite as often as they do around here. New jobs and employers have come into town. But not enough of them. Despite all efforts to turn things round, and there are a lot of very determined people trying to do exactly that and doing very dedicated and thankless work on behalf of the local community, the impression that a casual visitor gets isn't of a place that is successfully moving forward into a brighter future. The place looks and feels like the heart has been ripped out of the community. I walked over to the site of the old Enderley Mills and stared at the new housing development that had replaced it and you could almost smell the scent of all those changed lives that had disappeared along with the factories.

Lifestyles that were familiar have gone for good or ill. Even the trip down to the football isn't what it was. On the rare occasions when I was tempted to abandon my loyalty to watching Crewe Alex I occasionally went in the 1960s to watch Stoke City play. You stood on bare chilly concrete steps and felt very fortunate indeed if you could find an iron support railing to lean on so you got a clear view of the action. Now you get a nice seat and a brand new stadium but no kid can afford to pay the entrance cost out of a bit of pocket money. The ownership of most teams has become remote and disconnected from local experience. In the 1930s the owner of Newcastle's Enderley Mills was called James William Gibson.

He wasn't local. He came from Salford. So he put some of the money he made from the factory into saving his own local football team. It cost him £2,000 to rescue Manchester United from bankruptcy. Just before Christmas 1931 the now famous club was in such dire straits that it couldn't pay the wages of the players and was about to go under. Gibson stepped in to provide enough cash to cover that bill, buy the players a turkey and provide a stable guarantor for the clubs many obligations. Effectively he bankrolled the club and saved its existence for £2,000 and it then went on from strength to strength. Of course £2,000 was serious money back then. You could have bought 10 houses for the same money. Now you would be hard pressed to cover the cost of one player's wages for a year if you sold 10 average houses. The game has become remote from the experience of those who nourished it in the past. That doesn't mean that it has become worse. The standards are higher in virtually every respect, from the seating, the catering, and the behaviour of the fans right through to the quality of the performances and the excitement of the spectacle. But the feeling that the game has lost contact with its base is real enough and is another example of what communities like this feel that they have lost along with their industrial past.

The company that owned Enderly Mills was called Briggs Jones and Gibson. It went out of business in 1999. A remote holding company owned by international financial experts had taken over the business and they decided that they could make more money by closing the place and selling it off for housing than they could by modernising it and running it. That kind of change is hard to take. If you lose your livelihood because technology evolves it is bad enough. But if you lose your livelihood and your community goes into decline because no one is prepared to put enough investment into to modernisation in order to secure the future of a business that is perfectly capable of being viable then it must be very hard to take.

I walked away from Enderley Street and headed off to try and find the remains of the castle. I found it a mile or so away after a bit of a struggle. There wasn't much to see. Stuck behind the bins of a care home you could see an anonymous little mound of earth covered with brambles. It looked like it was a bit of earth that had been left over from a building project. Instead a sign proudly told me that it was the main remains of the old castle. The same sign steered me to cross the road and look at an area of the castle walls that had been dug up and left exposed. These were equally underwhelming. There might have been ten yards of foundations that never got above the current ground level. They were stuck at the end of a street of red brick terraced houses and looked like a bit of rubble left over from a recent demolition job. Way back in the 12th century this had been part of a genuinely important castle and before that there had been Roman settlements in the area. Gradually it had fallen into disuse and then much of the stone had been taken away to build a nearby foundry. Now all that remains of what was once the most impressive building for many miles is a tiny bank of earth and a few yards of foundations. It was not a great omen for the future.

****

Newcastle Upon Tyne's castle has fared rather better. The Keep of the castle stands proudly in the centre of town just next to the glorious High Level Bridge. It therefore occupies one of the prime sites in the city. A site that is so good it has been chosen again and again over the generations. The Romans built here. In fact if you look at the Ordnance Survey map you can clearly see two sections of Hadrian's Wall heading straight for the heart of Newcastle and meeting up within the grounds of the later castle. It didn't take long after I arrived there to figure out why. The Tyne is an impressive river with an even more impressive estuary. As you approach the sea, there aren't many spots where there is some good firm higher ground right alongside a narrower section of that estuary. When you make the hard climb up to the top of the Castle Keep you can look out across the water and see that here is the right place to put a river crossing. Go further downstream and the estuary starts to widen significantly. Go further upstream and the land adjacent to the river isn't so convenient to build on. This is the spot that any sensible ruler would select if they wished to control the river crossing, tax anyone coming across for trade and see off those coming with more threatening intentions.

I tried to trace first the evidence of Roman occupation. It isn't hard. Hadrian's Wall starts to the east of the city in a place appropriately named Wallsend. It is not the most romantic of settings for the start of the greatest Roman building project in the whole of Britain. It sits on some low featureless ground beside the old docks and across the way from some sheltered housing. Given how valuable the land must have been at the peak of Newcastle's industrial period it is something of a miracle that any of it survives. The other Newcastle decided to rip up its fine old medieval castle because it was in the way of a perfectly good foundry. The Tynesiders in the same period of industrial development were quite capable of doing a fair bit of damage to their own heritage. They ran the railway line through the middle of their medieval castle so effectively that I jumped back in surprise when I looked out from the fine windows of the Great Hall to find that a train was trundling past only feet away. The train line firmly separates the Keep from the North Gate of the castle - making the Victorians priorities very clear. Trade first. Heritage second.

When it came to the Roman ruins out to the east at Wallsend we have been a touch luckier with our collective inheritance. The developers put a road through it instead of a railway line. A busy 'A' road carrying buses, lorries and cars into the city along the line of the old wall runs right across an entire corner of the Roman fort. Someone clearly thought that a good road was a lot more important than the site of the start of one of the most famous walls on the planet. Nevertheless, a lot of the Walsend fort has remained remarkably well preserved. There are plenty of very fine ruins left to see - provided that you are happy to trace mainly foundations. As with all good Roman ruins you can find a bathhouse and some interesting plumbing. Here you also have the living quarters for the officers, the more basic living quarters for the ordinary troops together with plenty of evidence of gateways into and out of the complex. I trudged round the ruins very happily for a considerable period of time. It proved remarkably easy to get a feel for the scale of the enterprise. This fort may have been stuck out on the edge of the empire but it was an important place. The Romans built it to last and to a very firmly controlled plan. I quickly found myself imagining the hustle and bustle of all those equally firmly controlled troops moving about amongst the grid layout and getting ready for their next march out to more dangerous territory.

Then I headed out to the West of the city to see if I could trace the line of the wall as it headed out towards the high remote hills of Northumberland. Out this way the Roman remains were rather harder to find. The same 'A' road that goes past the Wallsend site straight into the city of Newcastle goes out the other side in an even more impressively straight line. It climbs steeply through what is now an inner city environment heading firmly towards the best defensive positions the Romans could find to put their border between barbarian lands and the empire. On its way upwards it passes a Hindu temple and more fast-food outlets than it seemed possible for any one road to sustain. All the way along its route this major road faithfully follows the old path of the wall but is sited a few yards to the north. Just past one of Newcastle College's many sites the map shows that there is a section of the old wall still intact. I could find no signs to help me locate it. Instead I had to rely on the good people from the Ordnance Survey who had kindly put a very large symbol of a Roman Helmet on my map to tell me what to look for. Unfortunately when I started to walk the obscure backstreets in the area indicated it was far from easy to find the precise spot. The Helmet symbol on the map was covering several streets and it was far from obvious to me which one to follow. I had walked past the line of houses surrounding the site twice before I resorted to the last strategy I normally go for and tried asking one of the local dog walkers. She looked at me as if I must be really stupid and said "Do you mean the Roman ruins over there?" and pointed twenty yards away to some railings and a sign.

A perfectly respectable area of Roman wall stood bravely near the top of the hill looking down over the Tyne. An idiot should have been able to see it. A couple of streets further away there was another section of ruins marking the spot where a second Roman road had run out across the wall over the Vallum ditch and further on down towards the Tyne. For a two thousand year old ditch it was still in a very good state of repair which was a lot more than could be said for the plastic signpost explaining what a Vallum was for. That had rotted away and was in such a poor condition that it was impossible to read anything it said. Which might be just as well. After years of reading about Hadrian's Wall I still can't find much agreement between the various experts on the purpose of this structure. Why build a deep ditch many yards behind the main wall?

Most sources do seem to agree that the Vallum was built after the wall was first constructed and many of them say that the ditch serves a defensive purpose.[14] Which is a bit odd given that it is on the south side of the wall which is where they were meant to be safe. This would suggest that the poor Roman soldiers weren't just trying to defend themselves from barbarians from the north but also had to fend off trouble from their own side of the wall. More plausibly this ditch may have been built to control trade routes and taxes more

---

[14] Roman Britain, Keith Branigan, (ReadersDigest, 1980) p 305

effectively. It is not a bad idea to keep the riff raff away from fraternising with your troops. It makes smuggling harder and on most borders this is every bit as important as preventing surprise attacks from people pretending to be friends. You don't want locals selling hot pies to your soldiers and chatting them up when those troops are meant to be diligently policing trade and staring out into the distance to check for enemy soldiers. Better by far to set up a military exclusion zone and mark it very clearly.

Either way it was easy to see that the Vallum I was looking at made a strong statement. If you cross this point then you are in the controlled military environment of the Emperor's wall and you've only yourself to blame if you aren't obeying the rules. Further to the beyond the city and out on the open moors you can see the remains of the wall standing proudly against the enemy but you don't always get to see the full depth of the Vallum or to fully appreciate its importance. Here in this part of the city it is a bit the other way around. It is hard to be impressed by the little bit of wall that is left surrounded by all these other buildings but you can see just how deep that Vallum ditch was and gain an understanding of how much effort it also took to build that.

Out beyond Newcastle there are plenty of bleak landscapes where Roman walls, ditches and forts become powerfully dramatic and impressive, especially when they cross open countryside at the top of steep drops. So it is logical to assume that the original starting point of the Wall in the centre of Newcastle must have been every bit as impressive. This crossing point was strategically important and worthy of their best efforts. The same logic was still working a thousand years later. When the Normans arrived they found little left of the Roman's efforts but they has no difficulty in recognising the importance of the location. William the Conqueror got almost exactly as far up north as the Romans had done before also discovering that it was more trouble than it was worth to try and hold any more land. He then established a bridgehead over the Tyne and decided that starting a war with Scotland wasn't a good idea and it might be much better to dig in and consolidate. Better by far to build a new castle at this point, control trade, and collect taxes exactly like Romans. So William put his son Robert Curthouse to the job and he put up a classic motte and bailey in 1080. As a business enterprise it worked remarkably well and so the new castle was constantly improved on for the next 300 years and the name of New Castle got attached to the community that grew up around and within the defences. This was a prosperous place where a lot of trade was done both by water and by land and an ideal point for transporting out hides or wool produced by the northern hill farmers and for setting up little production units in order to make goods to sell those very same farmers or seamen who came to do business. It was also a very dangerous place. Any self respecting army invading from the direction of Scotland was bound to see it as a very desirable target.

I went back to the castle to explore a bit more of the city centre. Walking away from it eastwards along the river front the city now has a relaxed feel to it. Instead of building walls to fend off unfriendly neighbours the current managers of the city are busy trying to build attractions to welcome them in. The river has moved on from being a smelly industrial basin where all sorts of horrible substances were washed away by the tide. Only for rather a lot of them to come back and stink the place out. It is now the sort of place where you seek out a cafe or sit out chatting at one of the "official relaxation stations" that the council has kindly provided. Apparently this is the new name for a couple of garden chairs and a table left out on the river front. You can settle down at one and eat your meal from the nearby Swedish deli if you are so inclined as you watch the river slide by. You can also get a pie from Greggs and do pretty much the same. All tastes and pockets are catered for. You can even, should you be sufficiently wealthy, park your yacht at the Newcastle City Marina and take in the view from the comfort of your own boat. On the morning I was there a strictly limited selection of the jet set had chosen to do so and I only spotted three modest little boats heroically moored right in the centre of the action. San Trope was clearly doing a touch brisker business but a brave effort had been made to at least try and use the water front as part of the efforts to rebrand Newcastle. It was one of many signs that the city is changing and mounting a pretty decent fight back against the decline of its traditional heavy industries.

A little way down the river perhaps the best known sign of this fight-back proudly spans the Tyne. The graceful curving arch of the Millennium pedestrian bridge takes you over to the Gateshead side and the triumphantly modified old warehouse of the Baltic Centre. Instead of storing huge quantities of flour in an ugly eyesore, an effort has been made to turn the place into a modern art gallery with an appealing cafe and generous exhibition spaces. Which I was very much looking forward to seeing and admiring. I happen to be one of those people who quite likes challenging modern art. When it is done well. When it falls flat I happily join in with those who think it is trite and uninteresting. On this occasion I was disappointed to discover that the main exhibition left me cold. There were a few brick walls plonked in the middle of a large hall with some huge photographs on the wall that I presumed were meant to bring the meaning of the piles of brick to life. Unfortunately the whole thing failed miserably. I used to work at a building college, teaching reluctant bricklaying students to improve their communication skills. Whenever I visited the areas where they were practicing their best work I was always staggered and impressed by the skills on display. After enough visits even a complete amateur like myself couldn't avoid developing a keen eye for sloppy brickwork with splashes of mortar stains down the bricks. That was precisely what had been dumped on the floor of the main gallery. I wasn't outraged by it. Or provoked. Or stimulated. Or uplifted. I was just bored and irritated by the loss of opportunity to showcase genuine local talent.

 At the same time as teaching bricklayers to improve their sentence structure I also had the opportunity to teach much the same thing to art and design students. They were not particularly impressed by my efforts but I was by theirs. The end of year show of any average regional art college is a fantastic opportunity to see imaginative art of genuinely high quality. I wished the curators of Gateshead's wonderful new gallery had taken a bit more trouble to visit their local colleges and acquire some local art and design work that really did challenge and stimulate the visitor. My personal reaction to what was on display was not positive. Nice gallery. Fantastic regeneration idea. Tedious artworks.

I crossed back over the beautiful bridge hoping that I'd just caught one bad exhibition in an otherwise successful programme. The city, and neighbouring Gateshead, deserve their regeneration efforts to work. Standing on the bridge itself you can see the new skyline that has emerged along the river bank and it very much looks to be a genuine improvement. New housing in cheerful designs has been carefully managed to ensure that the heights and the designs tie in well so that they mark out the great sweep of the river and stand as an advertisement for a determination to embrace an optimistic future. Instead of disused docks and an industrial wasteland there are attractive riverside developments and a deliberate transformation of the feel of the city. As I walked away from the Tyne uphill through part of a student residential quarter that impression of transformation was further enhanced.

Newcastle Under Lyme has plonked its students out of town on a segregated campus and so lost much of the benefit of the impact of all those young people. All it seemed to me to have gained from having the well-respected Keele University on its doorstep are a few soul-less drinking sheds. By comparison

Newcastle Upon Tyne has a couple of vibrant Universities and a hospital full of nurses right in the middle of the city. The benefits show. The streets were full of happy looking young people of all nationalities chatting in a whole series of different languages as they walked through the city. Perhaps as a result there were plenty of shops and cafes in the city centre all competing to offer something new and interesting to tempt you in. I had wandered round the town of Newcastle Under Lyme looking for somewhere to eat and been seriously disappointed by what was on offer. In the modern city of Newcastle I was spoiled for choice as I walked north through the shopping centre and out towards the older of the Universities. The city seemed younger and in a better mood than the town. Instead of out of town shopping experiences and out of an out of town student campus the city had got itself full of activity. New university buildings and new museums had helped attract new technology industries which in turn had also enabled attractive housing to be built.

The result had not been to dwarf the older parts of the city. It had been to enhance them and to integrate them into a complex place with many layers. There wasn't just the Roman city or the medieval castle to discover. There were very nice crescents and terraces of homes built during the peak of Newcastle's industrial prosperity. The type of places that might have suited the lawyers and the technical drawing experts that even nineteenth century industrialists had paid good money to employ. There were also some very attractive old University buildings where many of those professional classes would have been trained. And there were nice parks left to the city by some of the more philanthropically inclined wealthy industrialists. But these facilities would have been in a sorry state of repair If the city hadn't been earning its keep. It takes money to repair and renovate and respect old buildings.

In Newcastle Under Lyme too little of that money had been in evidence and as a consequence there were a lot of buildings from the past that should have been a credit to the place but were looking very tired indeed. Whether it was the shops in the centre or the big houses near the park most of what I could see looked like it was in bad need of a bit of tender loving care and an owner with enough cash to provide it. The town felt like it was in a state of decline and didn't quite know how to fight back. It didn't seem to have a coherent purpose about it or to show enough signs of progress. It was more like passing through a museum to the consequences of industrial decline. Too many people seemed to have found the future confusing and threatening and given up believing they could do much to shape it and it looked to me that there was just too much to fix for the efforts of those trying to change and improve things to be shining through. By contrast Newcastle Upon Tyne looked like it had plenty of fight left in it. If I had come as a student to Keele University I suspect I may not have been tempted to put down roots and to feel that Newcastle Under Lyme was the place where I wanted to use my talents. If I had arrived as an outsider and spent 3 years studying in Newcastle I suspect I would fall in love with the city and be very ready to stay on there and help it prosper. In a world of high technology and of knowledge industries these things matter every bit as much as the choices of location that factory owners made in a previous era.

The decline of traditional industries had been very hard on both places. There are plenty of dirt poor parts of Newcastle Upon Tyne where high rise flats dominate and some families have seen generations go by without any of the adults being able to hold down a job for any length of time. There are also plenty of former factory workers in the city and many skilled people hereabouts have seen their skills fall out of fashion and their earnings drop like a stone. There are, however, also plenty of signs that things are changing and that the city is quite prepared to re-invent itself again. My favourite sight on the whole walk came when I had nearly finished exploring and found myself passing an arch welcoming me to the city's China town. It was right at the end of a long stretch of medieval walls. You could walk for half a mile along 700 year old town walls and then within a few steps of all that history you could go under the arch into a busy streets of pungent smelling Chinese restaurants and food stores. It seemed to sum up the layers of the city. This is a place which has kept its past and seems equally determined to keep its future. It has been welcoming people in for a couple of thousand years and trying hard to turn them all into loyal locals. It was a very attractive combination and I went away feeling that I wanted to come back and stay longer.

Stamford Bridge

The two Newcastles have a lot in common with each other. The two Stamford Bridges don't. One is a football stadium yards from the busy Fulham Broadway tube station where football teams battle it out on a Saturday afternoon. Provided, of course, that the timing of the match fits in with the television schedules. The other is a quiet village near York where a proper battle took place. This particular Stamford Bridge is, in fact, the site of one of the single most important battles in English history. It was the battle that finally put the end to the constant threat of Viking raiding parties successfully pillaging the coast and much of the interior. It has, however, gone down in history as a fairly obscure conflict that is something of a footnote to the other major battle that took place in the same year. 1066 has a much more famous battle for us all to remember and that pivotal event has tended to push the other major conflict in that momentous year seriously into the background.

So I thought it might be fun to visit the site of the lesser known battle of 1066 and try and work out what actually happened there and why it mattered. I was fortunate to have the company of my friend Des, who shares a passion for history and eccentric days out. Des and myself arrived in the comfort of an eco-friendly saloon car on a dreary windy day in January to do our exploring. For King Harold and his rival for the throne Harald Hardrada the journey there was a little more difficult and the circumstances a lot more complex.

Hardrada came from Norway and was a Viking. To most people that immediately conjures up an image of tough marauders interested in little more than a bit of war, rape and pillage with a good session of drinking and boasting to follow. But he was considerably more sophisticated than that. By the time he arrived in England Harald Hardrada had lived in Eastern Europe, North Africa, the Mediterranean and the Middle East. He was therefore better travelled and more cosmopolitan than any of the other contenders for the English throne in 1066. His wife was a Princess from Kiev and in the 11th century that was one of the most advanced and cultured cities outside of China. Having made a lot of money and a strong reputation during his time as a mercenary and a trader across three continents he was clearly regarded as a perfectly respectable marriage partner for the daughter of a very powerful King. Certainly there was no problem over religious belief as Hardrada and his new life partner were both staunch Christians. On his return to his homeland with his up-market wife he proceeded to secure himself the throne of Norway and then set about looking for more.

The death of Edward the Confessor must have seemed to Harold Hardrada to be a very good opportunity indeed. So he struck up an alliance with the brother of his rival Harold, set off with significant numbers of very skilled warriors, picked up more in the Shetland Islands along the way and then probed the North East coast of England before finding himself a useful place to land at Ricall. Which just happens to be only 12 miles from the very attractive prize of the city of York. Serious efforts were made to defend the most important city in the North of England. Harold's best generals in the north and his very best troops were brought together to see off the challenge. Hardrada proceeded to beat them hands down in a hard fought battle and was then able to explain carefully to the occupants of York that they now had a simple choice. He could sack their city or they could accept him as their new ruler and send him a couple of hundred hostages along with a levy of men to join his army. Not surprisingly the good people of York decided that rustling up a detachment of troops was a lot less painful than having your family subject to the sharp end of Hardrada's army on a bender. The Norwegian King accepted their surrender and pulled his forces far enough back from the city to make sure it wasn't ruined. After all it was now his city and there was not much to be gained by making a mess of it. The rendezvous place where the new recruits from

York were to arrive was a crossing point on the Derwent called Stamford Bridge.

On a hot day in mid-September with the north of England nicely under their control the Vikings were feeling pretty relaxed. Miles away down south King Harold of the Saxons was preparing to fight off a Norman invasion and so there was nothing much to do but recover from the recent battle and wait for the arrival of a detachment of fresh men coming from the York direction. The only problem was that the Saxon Harold way down south had decided that the invasion by Normans wasn't absolutely certain to happen this late in the fighting season whereas the invasion by Vikings was already a reality. He and his best troops headed up north as quickly as they could via a forced march determined to deal with the threat that had already materialised. Historians give different lengths of time for this forced march. Some of them very implausible indeed. Wikipedia informed me that Harold moved his troops 185 miles in four days. In the days when I was very fit and ran marathons I once walked 35 miles in a day along the dead flat Thames footpath with a team of backup volunteers feeding the walkers. We were all completely shattered at the end. Even trained troops who had walked everywhere since childhood would not be able to walk that kind of distance, camp out, feed themselves, carry heavy military equipment and wear even the lightest of armour. The idea that Harold got to Stamford Bridge quite that quickly is therefore almost certainly wrong. Not if he wanted his troops to arrive in a decent enough state to fight a battle. Nevertheless, with significant amounts of horse transport, help from the local people along the way and fit well-organised troops they got there a lot more rapidly than Hardrada had even begun to think possible. It also didn't take Saxon Harold long to question the locals as soon as he got close to the York area and discover that his enemy was waiting in Stamford Bridge.

The first Hardrada knew of it was when he saw troops arriving in the distance. It is very flat land around Stamford Bridge and it is hard not to notice an army approaching. But it is also quite hard to tell the difference between a full blown army and a detachment of unwilling volunteers that you have been expecting to arrive from the same direction. For a while he thought he was seeing his extra men coming to join him from York. Hardrada had very little time to realise his mistake and react to a new situation. It was not a good one. More than half his troops were back with their ships. One of his first actions must have been to dispatch horsemen to tell these men to come quickly. But those re-enforcements wouldn't get there for hours. Meanwhile he had to face off around 6,000 very experience Saxon warriors who had come prepared for battle with whatever he could quickly draw together of troops that had been scattered around in the immediate vicinity. Most accounts talk of warriors rapidly pulling on armour and trying to organise themselves to stand against an enemy that outnumbered them by over two to one. Some historians think Hardrada's men had been just lazing on the river bank recovering from celebrating their last victory. Others have them strung out along a road marching towards York[15]. Either way they were not initially in any kind of organised battle formation and they were on the opposite side of the river from the direction that any re-enforcements would arrive.

Hardrada seems to have dealt with this situation with some skill. He pulled his forces into a battle formation, organised a defensive rearguard action, got the bulk of his army over a significant river, and did his best to hold out until help arrived. He seems to have made a major effort to try to hold the Saxons off at the river crossing. One of the most obvious things that strikes you when you visit the battle site is that this river was not an easy barrier to cross. It would not have been

---

[15] Michael C Blundell, The Battle of Stamford Bridge an Alternative Explanation, http://www.stamfor1d-bridge.dk/

good to have been caught on the wrong side of it with your backs to a river coming under pressure from ever larger numbers of unexpected Saxons. Nor would it have been easy to get either defenders or attackers across in the middle of a hand to hand fight.

When the account of the battle was written up a hundred years or so later a glorious tale of bravery was told about Hardrada's desperate attempt to get an army under attack across a river. We are told that one brave Viking of enormous stature stood on the only bridge and fought off the entire English army for a considerable period of time. Only for one very crafty Englishman to launch himself under the bridge on a barrel so that he could skewer the brave defender from underneath. It is a good enough tale for the sign board of the local pub to have a picture of it on proud display. Unfortunately it is almost certainly not what happened. There must have been more than one place where the river could be crossed, or the Saxons would simply not have been able to get enough people across to stand any chance of winning. Well organised troops could have held a single crossing point for a very long time unless they gave way to utter panic. Hardrada doesn't come across as a man given to panic. So it is almost certain that he was outflanked by troops crossing in more than one place. Whatever way it happened, enough English got onto the East side of the river for the Vikings to need to make a brave last stand with a shield wall, probably at the top of a short but awkward rise just above the river bank.

It almost worked. It took hours for the Saxons' superior numbers to wear down the Vikings. When they began to breach the barriers of shields held up by exhausted defenders Hardrada tried to rally his troops for the critically important task of re-establishing it. He died fighting to mend the breach. Saxon Harold's own brother then stepped forward to take Hardrada's place and fought on. Sibling rivalry ran deep in those days. He too was killed. Then re-enforcements arrived, almost, in the nick of time and the shield wall held for a bit longer. Had they been a little earlier they might have been able to tip the balance of the battle. Arriving late in the day they too found too many of their comrades had already been killed. They themselves became overwhelmed by superior numbers and were slaughtered in their turn. By the end of the battle there were no significant Viking forces left. Harold had utterly destroyed them. Reports say that 300 ships carried the Viking troops to England. Harold allowed them to limp back home in 24. He didn't have time to chase the few remaining forces because he had to rush back down towards Hastings where William had finally arrived. After an exhausting march and a hard-fought victory, not enough of Harold's best troops were in a fit state to make it back with him. So he fought and died at his second battle of 1066 with a different, and less experienced, muster of men.

Most historians agree therefore that the battle of Stamford Bridge did two very important things. It finished off the Vikings as a serious threat to Britain. And it weakened the Saxons sufficiently for William to beat them and conquer England and parts of Wales. So you might think that the battlefield would be preserved and afforded some considerable respect. Not a bit of it. Des and myself arrived to discover that every scrap of romance had been sucked out of the location. The town was split in two by a busy through road and we took our lives in our hands every time we tried to move from one side of the village to the other. Exploring the locality we came to the conclusion that the most likely place for the battle to have started, with the Saxon's taking the Vikings by surprise, is now a plastics factory. Moving on we then discovered that the most plausible site for the intensely contested river crossing is now a giant caravan park. They are very nice caravans and the site displayed a sign proudly informing us that it had won the David Bellamy award for conservation. But it wasn't easy to have your imagination fired up in a posh trailer park. So we walked on to try and find the location of the place where the last desperate serious defence might have been made around the shield wall. That was surrounded by a housing estate.

Which wasn't entirely a surprise. The entire town seemed to consist of a series of huge housing estates. One of them does at least try and pay a bit of respect to the history by having one of its streets named Battleflats Way. The estate consists of a series of very neatly kept front lawns, anonymous 3 and 4 bedroom homes and parked cars on driveways. If what you wanted was a comfortable home in a quiet crescent, then this would be a very attractive place indeed. If you were trying to conjure up important events from the past, then it was rather less successful. Nothing could have deadened our imaginations more completely and we struggled to bring back to life images of hand to hand combat of the most desperate kind taking place in this cosy environment. The next housing estate along leads you to a memorial to the battle that has been erected inches from yet another part of suburbia. This is where Hardrada made his last stand. Standing there we had hoped to be inspired by images of Hardrada constantly scanning the horizon in the hope of seeing his re-enforcements arrive. Instead we had a perfect view of two new housing estates that were being built on top of the last remnants of the battle fields.

Exploring the town simply took us from one era of housing development to the next. It seemed that for the past 30 years or so the good planners of the area had decided that Stamford Bridge was a very attractive place to live. On a river, just outside the lovely city of York, a few miles from the coast. What better place to raise a family? Or indeed what better place to make a lot of money by buying up farmland where a battle had once been fought and building as many family homes as you can possibly cram in before buying up the next plot of land and doing it again. Stamford Bridge had preserved a lot of very valuable history. Unfortunately it was the history of the excesses of town planners and building developers. It was not edifying.

After a series of fruitless efforts to find somewhere to walk where you couldn't see a housing estate we took a trip to the edge of town to see the local football ground. There was a beautifully kept pitch and the sound of local kids kicking a ball around for the simple enjoyment of it was a pleasure to hear. The pitch was, of course, surrounded by yet another housing estate. But it felt like the local kids were at least getting a safe, happy environment in which to grow up and were being helped to enjoy themselves by local parents and football enthusiasts who had a real love of the game or simply of watching kids let off steam and be themselves. The town may have been subjected to the worst extremes of building development running out of all control but at least there was one place around where everyone was having fun.

Football at the other Stamford Bridge is a rather more serious matter.

****

The last time I went to Stamford Bridge to watch Chelsea play football I had simply walked to the ground from my then home in Wandsworth, bought a ticket on the gates, and stood up to watch the fun. I hadn't got much money at the time, but the price was well within my budget. I turned up confident in the knowledge that I'd easily get in and wasn't disappointed. I had a clear view as my team Crewe Alexandra went one nil up with a soft shot and got very excited. I was rather less pleased when Chelsea equalised and my irritation was compounded when it became necessary for me and my fellow away supporters to be kettled up in the ground for half an hour to avoid being attacked by a notorious band of hooligans. I had strolled into the ground as a local resident on a day out. I was escorted from it behind a cordon of heavily armed police trying to prevent me from being torn apart by people I walked past every day. The Saxons aren't the only people who have suffered from an excess of testosterone.

When I tried to book a couple of tickets so that I could return to Stamford Bridge in Chelsea I discovered that things had changed. I needed to be a season ticket holder or to spend significant time and effort watching and waiting on line for the ideal moment to try and secure a rare treasure. The price had gone through the roof and the availability was even more problematic. Something fundamental had changed and the ground had moved heavily up market. No bad thing when it came to the troublemakers but very off-putting if all you wanted to do was watch a game. I decided that the only way to get a proper feel as to why it had changed so much was to arrive at Sloane Square tube station and to walk along the King's Road towards the ground, exploring as I went.

One of the first things I saw as I emerged from the station was a Rag and Bone merchant. Not a genuine one of course. It had occurred to some bright spark with a sense for marketing that it might be an entertaining piece of irony to call a clothes shop in one of the poshest locations in the whole of the UK 'Rag and Bone'. It was just across the way from both Tiffany's and Cartier's and it sold a range of up market women's fashion. Next to it there were a couple of up restaurants seeking to attract a well-heeled clientele. I tried looking in the window to see what was on offer but quickly decided that I might not have dressed quite smartly enough to hover around their premises for terribly long. I felt in more danger of being asked to move on than of being invited to come in and grace one of their tables.

None of this was particularly surprising. Sloane Square has been a place where the young rich go to spend money for a very long time and the only real change I could spot in the decades since I had last been here was that it seemed to be drawing in the wealthy from a lot more parts of the world. I headed off down the King's Road, parts of which had once had a reputation for being rather less up market and somewhat edgy and bohemian. An elderly friend of my wife lived just off it on the strength of a social worker's salary and a protected tenancy. For many years she rode a cumbersome tricycle up and down the Kings Road twice a day without anyone seeming to take the least notice of her eccentricities. Chelsea Registry Office had also once been thought of as rather different to the norm. If you were in the public eye and wanted to make sure pictures of your latest wedding appeared in the media then it was THE place to go in the 1960s and 70s. The quirkiness of the Kings Road back then meant that at the top end of the street there was a fair share of up-market establishments, but at the bottom end you were likely to come across punk rockers taking advantage of cheap rents to invent ripped jeans and safety pin face decorations. On a Friday night it was enlivened by a cavalcade of souped-up hot rods parading up and down the road whilst crowds stumbled out of the boozers to admire the spectacle. There was even a high-rise council estate tucked in at the gloriously named World's End. That end of the Kings Road was known as a place where a jumble of different social groups met to spend money and have fun.

The legacy of something special is still not hard to find. Part of the attraction is that one minute you can be on one of the busiest shopping thoroughfares in London and the next you are in a quiet residential back street. I took a turning off at Smith Street and walked around the block via Smith Terrace and Radnor Walk. The ambience completely changed. Inside a few yards I found myself walking past charming town houses which front onto streets that are not much use for through traffic. It was a real pleasure to stroll past top quality Georgian architecture built to provide comfortable family homes on the edge of town for people with a middle income. Admittedly there weren't many middle-income families living there now as the asking price averages somewhere around the ten million pounds mark. But many of the houses did seem to still be in use as large family homes and they still retained their large rear gardens. Some of the residents had chosen to place their living rooms upstairs and left the widows as clear as possible of clutter so that they could gain the maximum amount of scarce London light. Glimpsing through those windows I got the occasional sight of an immaculate interior laid out with what looked to me like all the ease of relaxed longstanding wealth. Living in the very centre of London has great attractions. Here one of the local parks is the amazing Chelsea Physic Gardens which possess one of the finest collections of obscure medicinal plants in the world. Go for a short stroll and you find yourself on the Thames embankment looking at house boats that are even more up market than the local housing. Instead of a local takeaway there is a "quirky gastro pub" that claims to be a "knick-knack filled update of a traditional pub". The choice of entertainment starts with the Saatchi Modern Art Gallery just down the street and never ends as you have on offer all the variety and change of one of the great capital cities of the world. And, of course, for work you have an easy tube ride into the city, into Westminster or into the top creative arts employment opportunities. This is the way to live well in a city. If you have enough money to carry it off.

As I walked down towards the bottom of the Chelsea Kings Road the very different feel of the street had not entirely been obliterated. Here the rents on shops were a bit cheaper and it was still possible to find restaurants and pubs that were making their money by serving large numbers of customers as quickly as possible with fun food and drink at reasonable prices. The World's End Estate was also still standing. This magnificently badly named high rise block had somehow managed to turn into a much sought-after location for affordable housing. Not many people feel that they have been despatched to the end of the universe when they have landed a home on a reasonable rental that is a few yards from the river in a posh part of town. There are a lot worse places to be offered a council flat. On one side of the estate you can find the Chelsea Muslim Community Hub. On the other is the Chelsea Yacht and Boat Club. It would be interesting to see the membership list and see how many people are members of both.

Walking around the World's End Estate, particularly at ground level, is an astonishing contrast from the experience of exploring the up-market homes that surround it. Back in 1966 when the design was approved it must have seemed a good idea to the architects to build in a solidly brutalist style and to get as many houses as they could in by building upwards. Walking the area today at ground level the attractions of the architect's vision weren't so immediately obvious. I just felt closed in and intimidated. Above me towered great chunks of concrete clad in brickwork. The walls seemed to loom up, which is not entirely surprising when you consider that 7 high rise blocks and 750 homes have been packed into a remarkably small space. The streets around the estate felt abandoned to cars and to car parks and I had the distinct impression that I was walking in places where pedestrians wouldn't normally go and weren't very welcome.

It was a lot more welcoming on the Kings Road side of the estate. Here a whole wealth of agencies were making an effort to draw in the estate residents and cater for their needs. Social Services was providing an Advice Centre. A Church had set up shop and was trying hard to encourage participation. As was the local Arts Centre. It wasn't entirely clear that either old time religion or radical experimental theatre were drawing in as much of a crowd as they would have liked but they were making the effort. So were the customers of the tiny convenience store and coffee shop right by the estate's main entrance. The Lisbon Delicatessen had bravely put out a couple of tables so that people could sip their coffee and eat custard tarts whilst imagining the feel of the Portuguese sun on their backs. It must have taken quite a bit of imagination in the February drizzle but a couple of brave souls were huddling under the sun umbrella doing their best to look relaxed and continental. Instead of joining them I walked past and tried one of the steel doors leading into the interior of the estate.

To my considerable surprise it opened. I had expected to find it locked against outsiders and for those without the right electronic switch card to be kept away. Instead I was able to walk straight inside and explore the interior of the estate to my heart's content. Above ground there are wide walkways that were designed to provide places where local residents could congregate and chill out. In many estates they turned into a nightmare location where out of control teenage gangs intimidated passers-by and made them feel distinctly uneasy only yards from their own home. Here they seemed fine. I leaned over the wall protecting the edge of one of the walkways and looked down on a local Primary School that looked very well-kept and was proudly informing the public that the school inspectors had declared their establishment to be outstanding. Then I walked on past the Over 50s Clubhouse to a central courtyard. The architects had decided that it would be nice to create a children's play area up on the first floor at the very heart of the estate where parents could chat, the over 50s could beam at the very young, and the kids could be easily and safely supervised. Unlike the brutalism of their building style this rather sentimental idea of the architects seemed to be working well. Instead of a hang out for drugs gangs it really did look like it provided a place where it would be easy to strike up a conversation, make some new friends and let your kids run off a bit of energy without worrying about London traffic.

In many parts of the country where the streets in the sky approach to housing was attempted it quickly became deeply unpopular. Few people wanted to live amongst such bleak and unwelcoming design. Even nice new kitchens and plenty of extra space failed to compensate for having to pick your way across stinking concrete walkways to make your home in a damp high rise. Sooner or later the estate became hard to let and had to be demolished. So there are very few places left in the UK where you can see fifty year old high rise blocks connected by skywalks that are still being lived in and still successfully attracting new residents. Something about living in the middle of the poshest part of town had compensated successfully for unattractive design and enabled the estate to avoid demolition and to prosper in its own way. I may not have found walking all the streets around here an entirely pleasant experience but there were plenty of signs that the estate was doing fine. It was achieving what it had set out to do. It was still housing a lot of people and doing so in a very convenient location.

Nevertheless, I was relieved to get away from the product of an arrogant determination to impose an architectural fashion on people who just wanted to be housed decently. I headed up Hortensia Road past the English National Ballet and Kensington and Chelsea College towards the Brompton Cemetery. Very quickly I found myself back into more affluent territory. All I had needed to do to explore the Worlds End Estate was just to push a door and walk in. That option was not on offer in any of the highly protected apartment complexes that dominated the outer edges of Chelsea that I was now walking through. The gated communities here had electronic security systems which firmly ensured none of the riff raff could get inside. Gardens and green space were shut behind high walls and were exclusively available only for those who could afford the astronomical cost of purchasing a little bit of quiet in the heart of London. In the beautiful old terraced back streets of Chelsea anyone is free to stroll about and admire the homes of the wealthy from close up. There is a degree of intimacy about it. Even a tramp can look at a King. In the newer developments that I began to encounter as I got close to Stamford Bridge there was a rather more determined separation of rich and poor. And the fashion for privacy and exclusivity was spreading. Work was underway on turning even more of the old feature buildings into well protected town homes that an estate agent could sell for a very tidy commission. The billboards outside the conversion of the old King's Library proudly proclaimed that it was going to provide "sophisticated individually designed apartments". It was clear that the new residents would have little difficulty sourcing their interior decorations if they did indeed prove to have sophisticated tastes. Inside a few hundred yards I spotted two shops selling chandeliers and an art gallery that wasn't making its living from promoting the work of the type of artists who starve in humble garrets. There can't be too many communities where the corner shops are competing to shift rock crystal lighting features at eye watering prices.

Yet within yards of all the new money and the walled off luxuries I found 39 acres of green space available to anyone who cared to explore it free of charge. Right next to Chelsea football club there is a gloriously protected bit of public space that anyone can stroll around at their ease. Admittedly it is necessary to share your walk with several thousand graves. But that is exactly what was intended back in the 1840s when the place was first opened. The creators of the Brompton Cemetery never wanted to create a place where death could be closed away and forgotten about. Rather they designed it to draw people in and allow them to feel comfortable as they shared time with those who were no longer living. Right from the start visitors were expected to spend relaxed time here amongst those they cared about who had gone before. With the passing of time the cemetery has gradually developed even greater character and become an even more attractive and interesting place to stroll through.

Provided of course that you don't like your environment to be too heavily controlled and organised. Almost the second you walk through the gates you find yourself in a curious mixture of carefully managed spaces and anarchistic ones. You can walk along wide clear pathways amongst long rows of classical columns and see stone angels, small memorial stones and great family vaults which have just about been kept quite neat and tidy. But you don't have to wander far to find large parts of the grounds where the graves have slid into the earth at eccentric angles and then been over-run by ivy and brambles. Here no one has got over enthusiastic about clipping back every last bit of natural plant life and so it is often hard to tell where a once highly prized family grave begins and ends amongst a confusion of self-seeded shrubs. A tangled mess of vegetation and stonework is jumbled together, allowing a substantial area of refuge for wildlife in the middle of the city.

Even the trees seem to have got out of control. They loom about above you and reach out great thick branches to take advantage of every last drop of sunlight. These magnificent specimens started out life as part of a careful plan designed by experts in creating interesting arboretums. Victorian designers tended to know exactly the right species to plant in order to soften and give added interest to a place where you came not only to honour the dead but to see the scenery and to be seen by society. Almost a couple of hundred years of growth has now turned their carefully chosen specimens into great monsters that were almost as hard to control as the most determined of the brambles. Crows squawked from their branches with menacing sounds that cut through the winter air and disturbed the silence.

To be honest there wasn't a lot of silence to disturb. The Brompton Graveyard may be a rare place of tranquillity in the midst of a major international city but it is not remotely a place of quiet. It is on the flight path to Heathrow and every couple of minutes a new plane comes in. As soon as the sound of one fades the next one begins to arrive in a never ending queue that lasts the full length of the cemetery's opening hours. In the distance I could hear the sounds of piledrivers working on a building project a little way off in the distance.

123

Then there were the usual sirens. And the sound of the tube line that runs along the whole of the west side of the plot. I had the place almost entirely to myself on this winter's afternoon but there was little prospect of forgetting that I was in the middle of a very noisy city.

I walked on past the golden stone chapel of remembrance with its magnificent grade 2* listed dome and headed deeper into the graveyard trying to find an entrance to the catacombs. Beneath the ground here there are great stretches of tunnelling in which many of the dead are stored. I knew that these sections were closed to the public and that plans were underway to make them safe and re-open them but I wasn't trying to get down there and explore the darkness. I was looking for a place where I knew I could get an unusual vision of the Stamford Bridge football ground. There is a point about half way along one of the colonnades of golden stone where steps go down towards iron railings that protect the entrance to one part of the underground storeroom of the dead. If you stand at the top of those steps you can look through a gracious arch and see the football stadium perfectly framed by classical architecture. It is a peculiar sight. You are in the midst of an eccentric jumble of decaying gravestones. Away from you stretches a carefully planned avenue of classical columns called the Great Circle that is trying hard to give formality, structure and unity to the heart of the cemetery. Below you a steep flight of steps leads down into the depths. Everything is redolent of the past and still firmly marked by the designs and the intentions of the Victorians. Then you glance up and through the gap in the archway you are staring straight at one of the most modern football stadiums in the world.

When it was first chosen as a suitable site for what was originally an athletics ground one of the main reasons Stamford Bridge was selected was that back in 1877 the land around here was fairly cheap. A few decades earlier that had also been a good criteria for choosing the site for a large graveyard. So it is perhaps not entirely surprising that the two places ended up quite so close to each other. It is, however, a real visual shock today to view the football stadium from the midst of the graveyard. The two immediate neighbours don't seem to sit naturally together. A casual visitor hoping to stroll around in the peace and quiet of a graveyard on a Saturday afternoon must find it strange and bizarre to hear the shouts of collective anguish or joy as Chelsea go about their business of entertaining the public. I imagine many of the club's supporters would be even more surprised to discover that this splendid graveyard sits right next to their club.

Inside yards of leaving the cemetery I was at the entrance to the Stamford Bridge in Chelsea. Or more accurately to the entrance on Fulham Road. I had expected to find both the football club and the burial ground something of an anachronism in the middle of such a wealthy part of London. You don't normally find untended wild space across the road from carefully guarded gated communities. Nor do you normally find a sports stadium in the posh part of town. But almost as soon as I started to explore the Stamford Bridge Stadium it became clear that it was not the football club that was out of synch with modern Chelsea but rather my own attitudes about what a football club represents.

For a start there were security checks on the gates even on a quiet Monday in midwinter with no match on. Two bored guys took a look in my bag and asked what my purpose was in wanting to visit. It bore a distinct resemblance to the surveillance you encounter if you enter one of those nearby gated communities. Apart perhaps from the lackadaisical way that the checks were conducted. I clearly didn't look much like either a terrorist or a hooligan so I was waved in. Then, once I got inside, it quickly became apparent that the football stadium had been smartened and dragged up market every bit as comprehensively as the surrounding streets. The first thing I encountered was a huge hotel. It didn't look like it was catering for cheap overnight stays for fans travelling up from backstreet terraces from the inner cities up north that had once supplied the bulk of support for the game. It was more the kind of place that you'd book for a business conference if you wanted to impress your clients and where you might accommodate your keynote speakers in order to reward them for jetting in from distant lands. The stadium offered a choice of places to eat that included a quality restaurant, a café and a tea shop. There was also no shortage of souvenir and branded clothing retail experiences. Only one was open on a weekday but it was a substantial and well-appointed store and when business became brisker a second store sat ready to open its doors and welcome in anyone prepared to pay astronomical prices for branded clothing. Everywhere I looked the ground was freshly painted in various tasteful shades of blue and giant billboards had been dotted around the ground to display high quality illustrations of the great players who had graced the club. If that wasn't enough to build your enthusiasm for the beautiful game then you could pay to get taken on the tour of the ground so that you could let your kids see the hallowed places where the teams changed and the tunnel that they used to run out onto the pitch.

Football has come a long way since the days when the residents of places like the World's End Estate used to pour out of their high rise homes or terraced streets, walk a short distance to some run down terraces and hand over a few shillings for the chance to stand together in a crowd and cheer on their favourites. Few residents of social housing can now afford to buy a ticket. For most working class people the standard way to consume the sport is to watch it on TV if they are lucky enough to be able to afford the subscription. Actual attendance at a match is the kind of lifetime treat that drives a horrible hole into the budget of a struggling family. For many people the cost of entry for a family of four exceeds their weekly income and once you consider all the competing pressures on disposable income attendance at a game just isn't an option.

But that group of people is no longer the core audience for the sport. The club has changed as its surroundings have changed. Stamford Bridge has altered every bit as much as the streets around here that have become up market gated communities served by corner shops selling chandeliers. It is still a place where a lot of people go to enjoy themselves. You just need a lot more money before you can afford to do so. Many of modern spectators only come here every now and then. You come in order to spoil yourself or your kids. Others come as part of the fortunate few who get an invitation to join the corporate clients in a hospitality box. The regular season ticket holders are paying out very good money for the privilege and, whilst few of them will have quite as much income as the owners of the most stylish Chelsea homes in the neighbouring streets, they do have to be generating a significant salary before they can afford to shell out. The club belongs in its surroundings. It reflects a wealthy locality and serves the needs of an affluent international city.

I sat in the very stylish football club café sipping my particular choice of coffee beans and nibbling on my selection from the very nice salad bar and wasn't entirely regretful of the change. It felt a lot better to relax in comfort at the ground, even if I couldn't get my hands on a precious match ticket, than it had to stand cowering behind a police line as they escorted me to Fulham Broadway station to protect me from being beaten to a pulp for favouring the away side. I decided that I like my battles of Stamford Bridge to be firmly part of history not something I am forced to participate in against my will.

Bolton

The first thing that most people think about when they hear the name Bolton mentioned is not necessarily leisure and recreation. The mill town in Lancashire made its name by being very good at industrial production during the nineteenth century and ever since then it has had a bit of an image problem. But it has never been the case that it was universally grim up north. All those mill workers wanted to enjoy themselves and it was usually only during mill week, when almost every factory in town closed, that most of them had enough time to spare to get on a train and visit the seaside. The rest of the time they needed somewhere more local to enjoy themselves and great efforts were made by decision makers and philanthropists to make sure that they had the opportunity to do something locally that was thought to be better for them than a trip to the boozer. Providing opportunities for good uplifting fun and healthy fresh air was widely seen as a really important means of ensuring the working classes were a bit healthier, a touch less rebellious and rather more religious than they might otherwise have been. Parks and gardens were the ideal choice. They also happened to be very popular and, as the voting franchise extended steadily during the nineteenth century, so did the incentive for politicians to offer local people something worthwhile to do with themselves on a sunny Sunday afternoon. Across the country towns and cities vied with each other to show that they could create a better park with a nicer bandstand and a better lake than any of their neighbours. The people of Bolton Lancashire were every bit as determined as anyone else to ensure that their leisure facilities were a source of civic pride.

So I wanted my trip to Bolton to be an opportunity to explore the town's rich heritage of parks, gardens and country houses. My friend, Des decided to accompany me. He was born and brought up in Wigan which is 10 miles down the road. He had never been to Bolton. Local hatreds run deep in these parts! We came in from over the moors to the north and headed first for one of the country houses that had come into public ownership during the 1930s. Between the wars many towns in the north of England acquired gems of architecture and the land that went with it. Those who had inherited more wealth than income struggled to cope with the demands of the modern world and death duties that weren't easy to dodge. Fine family estates ended up in the hands of local authorities who put a lot of effort into preserving them and making them available for the whole of the local community. Discovering and exploring a new one of these rescued treasures is almost always a pleasure. So we headed to Smithills Hall with high hopes of finding something interesting. It didn't disappoint. It is a glorious mess of a building. Most fine country houses have been heavily influenced by one or two of their owners and show a degree of consistency in the building styles. Smithills Hall just seems to have been added to bit by bit whenever a new owner had a few quid and the time and the need or the inclination to try something new.

The result is great fun. Bits of black and white timber construction from one era bleed in to stonework from another. You look at one window and it has large rectangular panes of glass framed by massive stone surrounds that mark the building out as firmly belonging to the nineteenth century. Then you go round a corner and find another one where the frames of glass are so tiny that they must have been made in a much earlier era when it was a real struggle to make flat window glass of any great size. It must have taken hour after hour of the time of a highly skilled team of glass blowers to produce and flatten these small sheets and then to make sure they were safely captured between thin lead strips and hoisted high up into place. In parts of the building the walls consist of hard red sandstone, because that is what was admired or was cheap at the time. Then suddenly the next section will be made out of huge slabs of dark millstone grit.

No one seems to have bothered over much about making sure the connection between the two sections was straight or of exactly the same height. If a room needed to be larger than what had gone before then they simply pushed forward the frontage of the building and if the next generation needed to add something a bit smaller then the building doglegged inwards. When they got to the roofline they simply followed the fashions and the convenience of their own time so that some of the roofs run towards you showing off huge heavy timber frames whilst from the sides great stretches of horizontal roof tiles from a completely different era run straight into them. Ancient wooden doors appear without any signs of still having an obvious purpose or having been used for many years. Bits of gables that are hundreds of years old face off against mock Elizabethan frontage which isn't. The whole jumble of shapes and styles might easily have produced an ugly mess. Instead it works brilliantly.[16]

Enough time has passed here since the last building work for each part of the structure to look like it belongs alongside its utterly different adjoining parts. There is nothing predictable about the building. Much enjoyment can be had by walking past the next corner and discovering that what meets you eye is not what you expected and seriously different to what you have just seen. Des and myself spent a deal of time spotting new bits of building that we couldn't make any sense of or date properly. This was not entirely surprising since it has been going through changes since the days of the Knight's Hospitalers and there is something remaining from every century since 1339 when it first entered private hands.

The gardens closer to the house proved rather easier to understand. The last set of alterations had created a charming terrace at the back which led you down to a lawn and then the sharp drop of a ditch marking the end of the domestic area. If

---

[16] For a proper detailed history see W.D. Billington, Smithills Hall, (Halliwell Local History Society, 1991).

the owners of the home required a longer walk then acres of pathways led off in each direction. We took one to the north and walked through an area of wild woodland. Or to be more accurate we walked through an area of woodland that had been designed to look attractively wild. Peculiar trees appeared that had clearly been brought into the country many years ago to grace the estate. Most of them had done their job of staying in their place, growing to an impressive sight and providing something interesting for us to look at on our walk. One of them hadn't proved so well mannered. Some of the pathways that led though the woods were almost clogged up by huge overgrown rhododendron bushes. Except they weren't bushes. They were fully grown trees. I have seen these plants growing in their natural environment high up in the cold mountain areas of India. They can stand up to blasting by the wind, scorching by the sun and soil nutrients being washed away by large amounts of rainwater. The worst that the hills of Bolton can throw at them is nothing by comparison and so the expensive ornamental specimens that were once so carefully brought across the world and planted here prospered beyond all expectations. They were now trying hard to take up every inch of spare ground and preventing any of the other trees from reproducing. So we picked our way through a woodland of old mature trees with groves of semi wild rhododendrons doing everything they could to crowd out and refuse sunlight to any young saplings.

Surprisingly it made for very pleasant walking. The heavy leaves of the invading bushes meant that you couldn't easily see what was just around the corner and, as a consequence, we kept finding ourselves constantly stumbling across unexpected sights. At some stage in history someone, probably the Victorians, had chosen to move huge blocks of stone down here and to use them to form their ideal image of a grove in the woods. A little further along the way we found further evidence of their work as rare ferns sprouted out from deep ridges in the bark of a tree and from between artfully arranged rocks in ways. Their plant hunters had been just as busy as their garden designers.

The original aim of the creators of this woodland park had been to provide the owners of the house with a delightful walk through land that looked wild and natural but had actually been carefully constructed and controlled to ensure that it contained all the elements of the picturesque. Since then the walk has gained a lot more wildness and become more genuinely picturesque and less predictable. The fortunate residents of north Bolton are free to walk across the carefully managed lawn behind the house, cross a valley of fantastic Victorian grottoes and then stride out across the open moors. Pleasures which were once the preserve of rich industrialists have now been made easily available to anyone with the ability and the energy to explore their own heritage.

We emerged from the complex maze of overgrown walkways and hidden grottoes onto a road that led to a farm park. Clearly quite a lot of local people were making sure their children also explored their heritage and someone was running a good business showing them where their food comes from and that it doesn't originate from a supermarket shelf. Or at least that is what I assumed took place in the farm park. We could only actually see a couple of plastic cows, a playground and some sheds and had to take the existence of real animals and real children on trust. We chose to turn away from the farmyard and head towards some old stables that had been associated with Smithills Hall. Relatively recently these had been hived off from the big house and sold for a housing development.

They seemed to have done a good job of gentrifying them. Not every old building can become a museum and those that don't can all too easily be left to decline into an unattractive state of neglect where they lack both charm and usefulness. Here the developer had put a lot of thought into converting the stables into top quality accommodation. Instead of knocking down awkwardly shaped features the builder had used them to enhance the appearance and the value of the new housing that had been created around them. Real efforts seem to have been made to match the modern building work sensitively to the skilful brickwork of the old. Instead of filling in the arch that horses once trotted through it had been turned into one of the centrepieces of the development and become a route into a central courtyard for a community of high quality homes. The sales office seemed to be doing good business. And it was not surprising. This part of Bolton seemed to have become very much the posh end of town. People who were earning good money in Manchester could easily commute here and spend their weekends walking the hills and the reservoirs. There is a network of small lakes, delightful valleys, woodland and moors stretching across the north of Bolton and amongst them a lot of very wealthy people have been very happy to convert old farmsteads, build new high end housing in local stone and transform the environment. A crude caricature of a typical resident would be someone walking their pedigree dogs around landscaped paths besides a charming local lake wearing a wax jacket enjoying the clean fresh air.

The great irony is that the things that make north Bolton an attractive place to live these days are exactly the things that previously resulted in some very dirty industrial activity being sited there only a hundred or so years earlier. Bolton was a bleaching town. Which meant that you needed a lot of water to wash the cloth. At first this was not so bad as much of the bleaching was done in the sun and the streams that came down off the high moors were scattered with washed cloth that had been left out in the sun to dry and whiten. Then technology changed and the bleaching companies discovered that it was a lot easier and quicker to use chemicals to treat the cloth. You still needed a lot of water, so a network of dams and reservoirs was created and the factories clustered where there was a reliable supply of water and near coal seams that provided cheap power. As a consequence quite a lot of muck and chemicals ended up in the local streams. To make things worse, as the factories grew in size and complexity smoke poured out from them. Some of it was coal fumes. Much of it contained residues from dyes and chemicals that were toxic. All this filth was being pumped out into valleys and into the air. The streams would not have been charming and the air would not have been fresh. Thirty six different bleaching companies had been working in Bolton at one stage[17] and the signs that they had been there could still be seen.

Over in the distance a giant chimney stood out on the skyline. We got back in the car and decided to explore what looked from a distance to be a real monster of a construction. We weren't wrong about the size. It was astonishing. A great chunk of masonry reared up in front of us and headed off for the sky. They'd built it tall and proud and put it on top of the highest convenient hill they could find. To give them credit they had tried very hard to get those bleaching fumes well clear of the ground in the hope that a cold day and a temperature inversion didn't send them straight back down to wreck the health of the locals. Now the chimney was virtually all that was left of a bleaching works that had provided enough money for its owners, the Ainsworth family, to acquire and improve Smithills Hall. Along with enough money to build another grand home on what is now Moss Bank Park. It was clearly no bad thing to be in the bleaching business in those days. Provided you got a larger share of the money than you did of the muck.

Peter Ainsworth, for example, started out as a simple apprentice bleacher after his father died in 1729 when he was only 7. It must have been a tough life because both his elder brothers and all their children died leaving Peter to inherit enough to be able to run a successful bleaching business on

[17] Bill Jones, Bolton's Industrial Heritage, Sutton Publishing, 2006, p41-46

his own behalf. Much the same happened to his uncle's children providing him with another significant boost to his wealth. He soon found himself the proud owner of a large factory, a comfortable home, several purpose built workers cottages and some very nice grounds. The business did well. His eldest son, also called Peter, decided, as wealthy sons do, that the home he inherited wasn't quite grand enough for his own children so he proceeded to build a fine country house in Moss Bank. Not to occupy himself, you understand. It was intended as a gift for his son Richard. Who in turn decided that he had enough money lying around doing nothing useful to acquire the very grand Smithills Hall that we had been walking around and then also not to bother to live in it.[18] The house at Moss Bank was much grander and more conveniently fitted out.

All of which left a fantastic legacy for the people of Bolton. Not only did Smithills Hall end up in public hands, the site of the grand home at Moss Bank with all its lands and gardens also became a public park. Along with the site of the factory. The giant chimney left over from the bleaching works is sat incongruously on the edge of one of the most popular recreation areas in the locality. The park seems to be doing a roaring business. It has swings, it has rock gardens, a miniature railway, a butterfly house, a cafe, wide open spaces to run around in and large areas of mature trees to explore. It also has a few ruins. Because the grand house is no longer there and all that is left are a few of the foundations. They have cleared away the memories of the past pretty comprehensively and the area is now completely different to anything its eighteenth and nineteenth century owners could have begun to imagine. Despite the looming presence of the chimney, it is now very hard to visualise this as a place where a very dirty business activity took place. Instead of workers heading into factories to earn hard won wages and early

---

[18] Billington, op cit, p 57-8

deaths the only thing that could be seen on the day that we visited was lots of young children and their parents rushing around having fun. The park isn't surrounded by grim industrial remains. It does have a busy ring road on one side. But on the other it has some very wealthy housing indeed. Once again what had been a tough working environment had been transformed into a pleasant area where locals could enjoy themselves. We were left with the over-riding impression that this part of Bolton had become pretty posh.

As we drove away along that ring road that impression didn't go away. We seemed to be continually passing through country areas where open spaces alternated with areas of homes built for those with plenty of money. Even when we turned in towards the centre of Bolton that didn't change. We came in from the West past fine housing, a prep school and then the one of the biggest and grandest public schools I have ever seen. A massive expanse of red sandstone is adorned with advertising proclaiming it to be the site of the best public school in the north of England. This is not the image of Bolton Lancashire that most outsiders hold.

Then suddenly, almost as if a knife had cut through the town, we found that we crossed a boundary. A couple of streets past the high end public school everything is very different. We turned off the main road searching for Bolton's main recreation park and found ourselves amongst what looked like some very poor streets. There were no wax jackets and pedigree dogs here. Instead we saw an elderly women trying to wrap her Asian clothing tightly around her against the cold as she emerged from one of the smallest of shops I've ever seen. It proudly proclaimed itself to be the Pak Store but it looked as miserable as its only customer. The streets here were of small terraced houses in poor condition that had been built quickly and cheaply for factory workers using ugly red brick that was starting to crumble at the edges. The first generation of factory workers had mostly come in from the surrounding villages rapidly transforming Bolton from a small location housing only 5,000 people in 1750[19] into what is now a town of 160,000. By the time that the last generation of factory workers was needed it proved necessary to recruit from Pakistan in order to get workers to do jobs that were no longer attractive to enough local people during the post Second World War labour shortages. Some of the descendants from that phase of migrant labour had prospered and moved out to occupy nice new homes on the edge of town and no doubt not a few of them were paying for their children to attend that very large public school. Others were still battling with the cold, poor housing, and low incomes in this neglected part of town.

Yet even the residents around here did have one excellent place to relax provided right alongside their terraced streets. Queen's Park in Bolton is a credit to Victorian planners. It has been providing local working people with somewhere very pleasant to enjoy their spare time for a hundred and fifty years. It is the sort of park that has everything you could want. It has a small river running through it so kids can drop sticks off bridges. It has plenty of play areas so parents from all parts of the local community can sit together and watch their little ones letting off steam. It has floral displays. It has a hidden amphitheatre where crowds once gathered to watch brass bands. And it has more statues than any self respecting park needs.

Strangely it only exists because of the American Civil War. Way back in 1861, as that confliect was just getting started far away in America, the Mayor of Bolton spoke to a meeting of operative bleachers to explain that in addition to their moral training the factory workers of Bolton badly needed something to improve their physical powers. Setting up a public park was, he said, the best way to help local citizens to be robust, happy and healthy. The speech went down very well with his

---

[19] Jones, op cit, p16

audience. But nothing was done. There was a cost involved and most of the rest of the local worthies weren't prepared to stump up the serious amounts of money that were needed to make their workers' lives a bit better.[20] But as the American Civil War wore on it began to have a very bad impact on trade. You can't bleach or weave an awful lot of cotton if there is a blockade on it coming out of the southern states that is being firmly enforced by Yankee warships. Imports of cotton to Britain fell from 2.6 million bales in 1860 to only 72,000 by 1862. Hundreds of thousands of Lancashire operatives, a high proportion of them strong supporters of Abraham Lincoln in the anti-slavery North, were placed on short time and then sacked.[21] By the time it got to 1863 the degree of the distress was so extreme that the national government felt it had to do something to help. A relief fund was established and this new source of cash together with the obvious desperation of the local working people was enough to turn around the opinion of local decision makers. The very significant sum of £50,000 got approved and in 1863 work got underway on the project. Unemployed workers were put to good use creating a park that they could then enjoy using in their free time. It opened in 1866 to great popular celebration by which time the cotton famine was over and the workers could go back to their regular trades. The park did exactly what its planners had hoped it would do. It saw people through the worst of a bad industrial recession and left them with a fine legacy of public works.[22] Working people could now choose to spend their Sunday afternoons promenading through some very attractive gardens with their wages in their pockets. No doubt not a few of chatted up their future life partners whilst strolling through Queen's Park.

---

[20] Bolton Public Library, local history archive

[21] Tristram Hunt, The Frock Coated Communist, Allen Lane, p199

[22] See Travis Elborough, A Walk in the Park, Penguin for evidence of how frequently and widely park building was used to as a scheme to help ameliorate unemployment e.g. p151

We tried to follow our own promenade without bothering about the chatting up bit. We crossed the river from the car park, skirted the edge of the children's playground and headed towards a sign informing us that the cafe was open every day. It was closed. So we explored the landscaped lake but had nothing to feed the ducks with so wondered off towards the old bandstand. This was even more heavily closed than the cafe had been. You could see a circle of land where in the glory days some very talented musicians had competed to show off their skills to huge crowds. You could also see bank after bank of circular terracing where visitors could sit and relax as they admired or criticised their efforts. The local history library has pictures of huge crowds assembled in this amphitheatre to watch people perform beneath a very attractive wrought iron bandstand. Des and myself found grass poking up through the terraces and nothing remaining of the garishly painted high quality ironwork. The park had a period when it had fallen into a very bad state of repair in the run up to the 1990s and it had taken a major effort by very determined local people and a good deal of lottery funding to get it back into a respectable state. The funding hadn't run to restoring the bandstand and the crowds were no longer there to support this form of 'uplifting' outdoor musical entertainment in an era of multi-media distractions.

The restoration team had, nevertheless, been able to a very good job with the floral gardens and as we got to the top of these we were able to stroll peacefully amongst them. Just below the gardens an attractive terrace ran almost the full length of the park. It was an ideal place to sit on a bench, admire the fine mature trees that cover the whole park and look out over the centre of Bolton and far beyond. This was the place that the locals had chosen as the ideal spot to dedicate a series of fine statues - each of them grandly surveying the view before them as if they owned the town. Some of them did. Others represented more rebellious slices of life. Local radicals had put one up to J.P. Fielding, a man who had done much to improve the conditions of local working people. The local Conservatives had then fought back by putting up one right alongside it to Benjamin Disraeli. He seemed to have no serious association with the town but they clearly felt people needed to have the influence of those dangerous radicals offset by providing a conservative hero for the public to admire. Then compromise appeared to have set in and the rest of the statues seemed to be devoted to people who had a lot less to do with politics but had spent a lifetime doing less controversial things like curing people's ailments.

Eventually we tired of reading inscriptions on statues or sitting on benches to admire the view and we worked our way back down to the car by crossing the River Croal. This river runs along the side of Queen's Park and then snakes its way around the edge of the main shopping centre before merging with large quantities of water coming down from the northern fells and heading out south as a rather more substantial waterway. Much of its route is now bordered by yet more parkland and nature reserves. We decided to finish our trip by heading south of the city centre to explore another part of the legacy of major recreation areas the Bolton is blessed with. We drove down to the whole series of nature reserves that run alongside the River Croal on the south side of Bolton.

They proved interesting but less fun. Perhaps it was because by this stage the day had moved on from a lovely bright, clear and cold morning to an overcast grey afternoon. Perhaps it was because there were huge areas of land to explore and we had begun to tire of walking. Nevertheless, I couldn't help thinking that one reason the area didn't exactly exude charm was that it hadn't really been given over to wildlife, walkers and horse riders entirely in order to protect the environment. Much of the area had that sad look that land gets when it has been used heavily for industry and commerce and has now become too worn out to be of much use for anything other than wasteland. It felt like we were walking through some valiant efforts to make the best of a seriously damaged landscape. I couldn't escape the uncharitable thought that it was going to take rather a lot longer before those efforts proved fully successful. There was a lot to clean up and we kept coming across evidence of abandoned activity which might very well be of interest to an industrial historian but seemed to me to be rather tatty. There is a long way to go to achieve the sort of transformation that had been achieved on the affluent side of town. As is so often the case, there had not been sufficient money around here to really do justice to the scale of opportunity this large area of protected land represented for those living nearby. Instead we kept finding ourselves trying to pick our way across footpaths blocked by great stretches of mud that took us through trees that had grown up quickly like weeds.

When we emerged we found our way to the highest remaining part of the Machester, Bury and Bolton Canal. This once ran right into the middle of town but right now it stops well outside next to a major dual carriageway. The current terminus is in a large basin that could easily have been transformed into an attractive leisure area. Instead it has the feel of something abandoned. The land alongside the canal had once been used by chemical factories. All the bleaching work in the town created a pool of expertise in the use and the production of chemical dyes and that created another whole area of industrial activity for the town. The land we had been walking through had once been the site of the manufacture of sulphuric acid, soda, coal tar and town gas.[23] No surprise then that the environment was taking time to recover. The Nob End Nature Reserve turns out to be the remains of a tip for toxic alkaline waste. The Moses Gate Country Park is a former site for paper making and is riddled with former coal workings to add to its own share of disused chemical waste. Most of the pools and waterways that were

---

[23] Jones, op cit p 73

trying to attract water birds and wildlife were old coal working hollows and many of the hills that had been thickly colonised by thickets of uninteresting trees were former waste dumps. The trees and scrubland provides homes for much wildlife and many people no doubt get a great deal of pleasure out of the opportunity to walk along networks of different pathways that stretch for lengths few towns can match. Nevertheless, if I am brutally honest, my own impression of the whole area was that it didn't feel much like a genuine wildlife sanctuary or an urban country park. It felt like an area that has been abandoned because it is too polluted and too close to a river that might flood for any housing developer to wish to clean it up. I came to the conclusion that it had been handed over to the wildlife experts, the walkers and the horse riders not because it was a rich and generous environment in which the local wildlife could prosper but for exactly the opposite reason. I became convinced that the land had been so very badly messed about with that no could think of another viable use.

To their credit the local community is doing its best to make something worthwhile out of that legacy. But to the outsider it looks like there isn't sufficient money for them to be able to do the job anything like the way they might wish. The transformation which seems to have been underway with considerable success in the north of Bolton has proved a lot more difficult here. We had begun the day by taking great delight in exploring the amazing legacy of leisure and recreation facilities and the fascinating history that goes with an old industrial town. We ended it happy to scuttle away to the car as it started to rain on the desolate remains of blighted land. Not every area of land that humanity messes up is easy to restore and revive.

****

When it comes to interesting places to take the family at a weekend the railway has always been crucial. If you lived in

Leeds or Bradford in the nineteenth century then there were plenty of places you could get out to on a day trip if what you wanted was to see some genuinely countryside for a change. One of the best options was to hop on the train to Skipton via Ilkley and get off at Bolton Abbey. There you could walk the banks of a beautiful stretch of river and reach some of the most stylishly distressed ruins in the country. It became a hugely popular way to spend a Sunday afternoon and a day trip to Bolton Abbey remains hugely popular.

These days most people get there by car. There is still a railway. A very nice volunteer operated steam railway. But it doesn't go from Ilkey and it doesn't reach Skipton. The line got axed by Dr Beeching and only part of it is currently operational, despite the best efforts of some very enthusiastic volunteers. You can take your kids on a nostalgia ride from Embsay to Bolton Abbey but then you have to turn around and go back again because neither end of the line is connected to anywhere else. Unless you count a tiny little miniature railway at the Bolton Abbey end. In its heyday thousands of people would get off at Bolton Abbey station and think nothing of walking the whole family two or three miles just to get to the start of the most interesting sights. Nowadays it isn't just the lack of walking practice that prevents most people from following that route. There is a fast and dangerous road between the very nice station halt and the river Wharfe. Few people would willingly walk their children across it.

I also dodged the fast road and began my walk near the old bridge over the Wharfe. It is a good looking bridge and a good looking river. The Wharfe here does what all self-respecting rivers should do. It meanders stylishly through a well-shaped valley and periodically slides down a few gentle shallow rapids. It is a broad and a pretty river and the path that runs alongside it takes you away from the traffic noise and towards the ruined Abbey that draws so many tourists here. I took a route that avoided a wide bend in the river and found myself

143

working straight through a field of sheep. There were little ridges and furrows in the field that stretched across the path so that every few feet the path took me over a slight hump only for it to go down again a couple of yards later into a dip. Row after row of these little ridges run the full length of the field and down towards the river. They are part of the old field system which allowed local farmers to grow rye, barley and vegetables on ground close to the river that had a nasty tendency to be too damp but also provided some very fertile soil as a result of centuries of flooding. The ridges kept your crop high dry and safe when the furrows were drenched by heavy rain and if conditions were different the roots of your crops found their way deep down to look for the last remaining drops of water in any drought.[24] So they were an ideal way for a farmer with not much machinery to get a decent harvest in all but the very worst of conditions. In most parts of England the evidence of this widespread practice has been ploughed out but here the sheep have been grazing the fields for so many years that the old field systems are intact.

There is more evidence of ancient land use patterns as you get further up the valley. Just round a bend in the river you start to see the buildings of a huge religious community rearing up in front of you and guarding the entrance to the narrower less gentle parts of the Wharfe valley. It is easy to get distracted by the scale of what lies before you and miss some of the signs on the ground of how the community was able to survive, prosper and construct such amazing buildings. As you approach the ruined buildings there are some rectangular pits in the ground that are perhaps forty yards long and twenty feet deep. They are dried up fishponds which the monks used to rear food for a Friday or for a period of fast. This is the clue to everything that happened at Bolton Abbey. The canons who

---

[24] It is frequently asserted that ridge and furrows were a simple by-product of ploughing. I believe the main reason was that arable crops can be grown more reliably with this field arrangement.

lived here weren't just good at religious ceremony and building for the glory of God. An important part of living in this dedicated community of enthusiasts was a desire to work hard to achieve the best with their land. Their theory seems to have been the desperately simple one that God has a rather strong tendency to provide well for those who work hard and provide for themselves. So this was a place where the latest and the best organised methods of food production were developed and used.

When a group of people work hard and dedicate their lives to a communal cause it usually produces a very healthy surplus. The Augustinian canons who lived at Bolton Abbey were no exception. They had started out with a small establishment at nearby Embsay. Strict discipline, long hours, effective organisation and a well-educated workforce got them a good reputation and it was not long before their efforts were rewarded with a gift of land along the river Wharfe that just ached to be developed. The Victorian day trippers were often told that the woman who granted the land did so because her son had drowned in the river. Which was a good romantic tale that had only one serious flaw. The boy was still alive when the grant of land was made.[25] He no doubt burst with pride at his mother's act of piety in handing over a substantial chunk of his potential inheritance. Or, alternatively, if he absolutely hated the idea and wanted it all for himself then he was powerless to do anything about it. Either way the land went to the abbey regardless of his opinion.

In the 1150s the community shifted to this new site. They immediately set about developing it with every bit as much energy and determination as they had displayed in Embsay.[26] Building after building went up, each of them seemingly more sophisticated and ambitious than the last. They had a bakery, a brewery, a shoe making workshop, a wool processing facility,

---

[25] Bolton Priory, Hamilton Thompson, (Thoresby Society, 1928)p 60
[26] Ibid p56

healthy supplies of vegetables and meat. Along with plenty of fish from both the river and those specially constructed tanks where they could be fattened up and kept fresh. They acquired holdings of land from parishes many miles away and the income and obligations to go with them. So they housed travellers, looked after the sick and the pious 'deserving' poor, educated sons, maintained a lot of local records and kept up high standards of scholarship.

All that success brought its own problems. It is one thing maintaining discipline and good order in a small community of highly committed individuals who have joined out of extreme religious dedication. It is quite another thing holding a community together when it owns very considerable assets and has become rich and powerful. People join safe and wealthy establishments for different reasons to those who join poor communities of sacrifice. They also battle for leadership and influence with rather more determination when there is an impressive asset to control. Even early in its history Bolton Abbey began to be beset by arguments and strife. In 1267 the disputes were so bad that the prior was removed from office and a new one put in place. An investigation into goings on at the Abbey by the Archbishop of York had found:

* "that the whole congregation took an oath and conspired

* that the cellarer is of no great profit in his office

* that silence is not well kept in the church

* that the infirm brethren are not well cared for

* that a professed novice does not repeat his service in the order by heart

* and that often after the convent have had its meals the cellarer and subcellarer regale themselves apart with more sumptuous meals than the others"[27]

146

To add to the concerns it was also found that the place was £324. 5s. 7d. in debt to neighbours. A serious amount of money in those days. So the old prior was made to take himself off to "some honest place of retreat" and a new one was elected. The fresh regime found it necessary to "utterly forbid drinkings and meals which tend to luxury and wantonness together with any disorderly conduct"[28]

A couple of hundred years later things seemed even less like our usual vision of a monastic style of community. In 1482 the Archbishop of Rotherham removed the prior temporarily from his duties because "out of the light heartedness of his heart rather than evil intent" he had loaded the house with debt and was guilty of "vain and immodest amours with suspect women."[29] The Archbishop was clearly a forgiving man. So forgiving that he decided to return the very same prior to his duties within two years. Apparently the establishment went downhill during his absence. I like to imagine that the Archbishop decided those suspect women were rather more helpful to the community than complaints about immodesty. I am less sure that the people of the time would have taken the same view or that the Abbey was maintaining the same fine local reputation for hard work and high moral standards it must have held when it was originally gifted the land. All of which goes a long way towards explaining the attractively ruined state of repair that the Abbey is in today. Henry the VIII could not have taken on the power of the church, seized its lands and defied the pope if the owners of places like Bolton Abbey had been universally popular. The Black Cannons proved exceptionally capable builders and in most years no doubt their order operated smoothly and efficiently. But it does not appear that they were well liked. Their purchase legers certainly don't indicate a life of strict self-denial. Even in

27 Ibid p63-4
28 Ibid p73
29 Ibid 109

1298, at a time when the place was growing in power and authority, they spent 55 shillings at Boston on saffron, pepper, galingale, cinnamon, almonds, rice and sugar.[30] This was over 4 times as much as it cost them to build a small house in Carlton. Relative prices may well have been very different in those days but it takes an awful lot of very luxurious meals to eat your way through four houses worth of exotic spices!

In 1539 they got their comeuppance. The whole operation was disbanded. All the assets were taken off them and, in an incredible act of waste and vengeance, the vast majority of the beautiful buildings, which had taken so much time, care and money to construct across 400 years, were deliberately put beyond use and left to rot. The Abbey may have had its periods of corruption and incompetence but it also did some genuinely good work for the poor and needy. One ruthless King proved to have all the resources he needed to put an end to both in one giant act of destructive suppression.

All of which left some very desirable property to be disposed of to friends and supporters of the King. At a price that provided very welcome income for the king and an excellent buy for the new owners. Some of the land and privileges that the Abbey owned in local villages were sold off separately in at least three significant tranches that brought in hundreds of pounds. The remaining part of the Abbey's possessions were then sold off for £2,490. 1s. 1d.[31] No wonder Henry was keen on dissolution and that Thomas Cromwell, the prime organiser of this enterprise, refused to accept the offer of £10 a year to persuade him to go somewhere else and wreck buildings. A few canons got small pensions but after flogging off the lead from the roof there still a very tidy profit for the exchequer.

---

[30] Idib p 122-3
[31] Idid p 114

The descendants of those who bought the land that had once been owned by the priory still own it and as I approached the Abbey ruins you could see one of their 'modest' second homes standing large and proud behind a wide sweep of very well kept lawn. Somewhere along the line one of the ancestors had decided that what any decent country mansion needed was a castellated roof line. They had succeeded in showing off a talent for wealth and extravagance but had left the building looking distinctly odd. It looked to me like a monument to bad taste. By comparison the one religious building on the grounds that Henry's henchmen didn't destroy remains exceptionally impressive. Somehow the locals here were able to persuade the demolition team to leave them one part of the abbey to use as their parish church. It makes for one of the grandest parish churches in the country. I am not a religious person but every time I have ever entered it the sense of being in somewhere sacred immediately impresses itself upon me with full force. This isn't a product of the piped choral songs that someone has decided to run on a constant loop in the hope that it will add to the atmosphere. This building doesn't need any cheap tricks to work its magic.

You, the poor sinner, have to enter it beneath a giant gateway which immediately starts to put you in your place and convince you that you are of very small consequence indeed in the universal plan. Once inside you find your eyes relentlessly drawn towards the place where the correct appointed authority stood. One of his main jobs was to re-enforce the message that it was important to submit to the will of people who could construct something this wonderful. Part of that wonder is provided by great chunky pillars that march their way forward supporting a roof so high that sound echoes gracefully. This quickly discourages you from disturbing the sound quality with your own meaningless casual conversation. In a building like this only important words are worthy of being spoken and those channel perfectly down the aisle. If sounds can mix and meld with light then this is a place where it will happen. Tall windows reach almost the full height of the walls enabling the subtle shades of the stains in the glass to flow into the building and move about whenever the wind moves a cloud across the sun. I sat for a while, as I almost always do when I come here, and enjoyed soaking in the atmosphere. The only other people in the building were a couple of local parishioners quietly making sure the building was tidy and the flowers were as fresh and spectacular as their usual high standards. The echoes of their occasional whispered conversations simply added to the atmosphere of respect. This is the kind of place that makes it easy to visualise the power of religious orders. This one remaining building is perhaps only one tenth of what was built here. If the rest was anything like as grand then in its prime it must have been a staggering place.

It still is. Outside I turned right and walked down the side of the building towards the river. The path goes through an old graveyard. A designer graveyard. It is the kind of graveyard that any gothic horror film maker would love to recreate. Slabs of stone have sunk into the earth at eccentric angles and the messages upon them show signs of a great deal of time and weathering. Several are covered in moss and lichen. Once you pass by them you get to the main ruins which are picturesquely situated on a broad sweep of the river. It is fascinating to walk through the remains spotting the signs of the past. Fireplaces and chimneys seem to have been far too much trouble for Henry's wrecking crews to bother with. But incredibly there are still some fine high thin walls standing, containing expensively carved window stones that would have been relatively easy to knock down and cart away. Instead they took the roof and left them to the elements. Clearly there was no good local market for church window stone. Or at least not enough of one for everything to have gone. There are parts of the ruins where years of the canons' best building work has been stripped away right down to the foundations and all that is left is a few worn sets of foundation stone for children to climb over and jump off. There are others where you can stare up a hundred feet or more and see where the roof line of long lost buildings once cut into the wall or spot a line of support stones marking an area where beams had once supported some structure.

The real beauty of the ruins at Bolton Abbey is not, however, the buildings themselves. It is the position of them. The canons picked the perfect spot. The Wharfe has a tendency to create flat terraces as the river cuts down a little further and the old flood plain is left standing high and dry. Here a fine meander of the river passes just below one of them and the canons did a great job of using the natural lie of the ground and then enhancing it. The result was they were able to create a good solid building platform safely above any risk of flood right alongside an unpredictable and powerful river. This means that almost from whatever angle you choose to look at Bolton Abbey you get a great view of the river counterpoising the ruins. My own favourite comes just after you cross the river so I walked down from the ruins and took the modern footbridge over the water to refresh my memory.

On a sunny Sunday afternoon one of the favourite pastimes for the modern visitor to the ruins is to stand on the footbridge at Bolton Abbey and watch people trying to cross the river by the alternative method - the stepping stones. I've seen people carrying babies pick their way across the erratically shaped and slippery stones to take them over the river this way for a bit of fun. I've also seen people try it in high heels. Usually if you hang around long enough on a busy Sunday afternoon in summer someone will fall in and the worst I have actually seen happen is that they get their legs wet and a bit of a shock from the cold. This is usually enough to provoke a scream followed by a lot of laughter. Though admittedly more of the laughter tends to come from the people on the footbridge than from the person who has just misjudged the distance to the next stone and lost their balance and a bit of their dignity.

Today no one was braving the stepping stones. The Wharfe was running just high enough to cover the top of them and then running rapidly beneath the footbridge and over a sudden sharp drop. You could feel the power of the water as a brown wave collapsed over the edge of the rock that had been supporting it and fell a few feet before carrying on down the river. The water continuously moved and reshaped itself and was a rich dark brown shade mixed with flecks of white. All the peat on the moors it comes off give it a strange depth of colour and at times there is so much lanolin in the water that there are soap suds on its surface that have nothing to do with pollution but much to do with soil erosion. It is easy to stand almost hypnotised on the bridge watching the water surge, change and flow. But the colour of the water isn't entirely natural. Too many of the local moors have been cleared of trees to make way for sheep or for grouse shooting and so the peat rapidly erodes and runs down the river. Despite this it is still a hypnotic activity to stand and see all that coloured water sliding by.

I tore myself away from this restful activity after a short while and crossed over to the other side. There is a delightful little sandy beach exactly opposite the Abbey where crowds of visitors like to sit with their kids and take in the curve of the river framing the ruins. It is the sort of place where it is almost compulsory for parents to try and teach their children how to skim stones into the river or persuade them that a bit of paddling in cold water is a great way to enjoy yourself. On a cold morning in February no one was braving it. I headed off up the river following a path that climbs quickly and gives great views of the valley as it starts to close in.

At the top of the rise a low sun cut through the trees and projected my enormous shadow across the river and onto the opposite bank. I was walking through trees watching my counterpart stretched out a hundred feet below me. At times it was cast onto the trunk of a nearby tree so that it was short and small whereas at other times I could see the full length of my giant shadow walking up the valley. That shadow was not my only company. In most tourist spots it is remarkable how quickly you can get away from the crowds by walking a very short distance. Yet here today there were plenty of other people out enjoying a good long walk. The first ones that passed me strode with great sense of purpose and seemed determined to cover their miles rather than take a bit of time to notice their own shadows moving below them. I suspect they also missed the buzzard circling high above, the rattle of a woodpecker and the huge heron hunting in grass that I came across a mile later.

The path curves briefly away from the river and goes onto a quiet country road just at the point where it fords a stream. A couple of motorcyclists gingerly picked their way over the ford, trying hard not to lose their balance and fall in as they rode across wet cobble stones covered by six inches of moving water. Fortunately it is not necessary for walkers to follow them and a very convenient dry route has been provided. Once you are over the stream it is a simple job to work your way back down to the river and cross the Wharfe again via the footbridge at the Cavendish Pavillion. Here you can see signposts directing the walker further up the valley to the Strid, where it closes in so tightly that it could almost be crossed by a single stride. Trying to do so is seriously unwise and it is not so very long since a young couple drowned on this section during what should have been their honeymoon. There are also signs inviting you to walk up the Valley of Desolation and discover the delightful little stream that falls over a series of waterfalls as it works its way down to the Wharfe from the high hills. Over a hundred years ago an extreme storm blew down hundreds of trees as the wind forced its way up the hillside and the name of the desolation it left has stuck long after fresh trees have taken their place and grown mature. The paths to wherever you decide to go are well marked and well maintained because this is still one of the busiest places in the whole of the Dales on a Sunday afternoon.

As I followed the signs back down the river towards the Abbey to complete my circuit I was walking past the cafe, the tourist shops, and public toilets where it was necessary to put up signs asking people not to wash their walking boots in the hand basins. They are right alongside the main car park that is used by visitors to the river and even on a cold winter's day it was doing brisk business. Anyone who wished to walk down river along its banks had no choice other than to do so by making their way through a car park for fully half a mile. It is easy to be irritated by all these cars cluttering up the banks of one of the best stretches of river in the country. It is also easy to forget that for a lot of people this is the only way that they can get to see such beautiful countryside. There are very few places in Britain where you can drive a car right up to the banks of a significant river and happily get your picnic out and relax. If you are disabled or you are too elderly to move easily this is just about the perfect spot. It is also an excellent place for a family to come and have all the supplies it might need easily on hand of nappy changes, food, fold up chairs and balls for the dog to chase. If this car park has replaced the train to Bolton Abbey station as the main way of getting the kids out to see the river and learn the pleasures of being out of doors instead of sitting at home playing computer games then perhaps it is an acceptable price to pay.

I did my best to remind myself of the service this car park was providing as I trudged past it back towards the Abbey. Just as you get close and think that this bit of the walk is over you discover that the wide flood bank that you have been walking across comes to an end and the river digs in to the side of the valley as it makes a sharp curve. It was necessary to walk across a wet field and climb the hill in order to get onto a road that takes tourists away from the depths of the Dales. A little way along this the road narrows to pass under an old aqueduct with two stone arches. The tourist buses can just get beneath the main one if they take it very slowly and steadily. The pedestrian arch is even less generous. Walkers have to duck to get under it and then you are back beside the remains of the Abbey buildings and the tourist shops that cluster around another car park.

The shops have been done well. The cafes are nice, there is a second hand bookshop, a whole food store, and a place where a tourist can browse a while and buy knickknacks and souvenirs. The current owners have taken every opportunity they can find to set up business opportunities around the Abbey. Within a couple of miles of it you can find a natural wood turning shop, a busy children's farm park, a camp site, very fine office space, a posh hotel and a restaurant. The resource of all this natural beauty accompanied by some very fine ruins has been worked and managed every bit as intensively as any agricultural field. But to give the current owners their due they have used the income from all those facilities to help maintain the area to a high standard and they have tried hard to tuck many of the businesses neatly away and to ensure that what they do contributes to the enjoyment of a visit instead of ruining it. I was tempted to rail against the evils of commercial development ruining a very fine beauty spot which our Victorian ancestors had enjoyed in all its simple splendour without a car being in sight. Instead, as I walked the mile back to my own car along the busy road, I just reflected on how things always change. It is perfectly possible to ruin our heritage by excessive and badly planned modern development. It is also perfectly possible to do a good job of trying to enhance and protect that heritage as you modernise it.

In both of the Boltons that I visited they seemed to be doing a half way reasonable job of achieving that.

The Dee – Wales and England

It isn't always easy to decide where a river ends. There is a case for saying it is when fresh water first starts to encounter sea water and turn brackish. If that is so then the first River Dee that I wanted to explore ends at Chester. After that it becomes a canal that runs straight down between controlled banks into the Irish Sea. There is, however, an equally good case for claiming that it actually ends far out in that sea. Great quantities of the silt that the river brings down from the Welsh hills ends up there and the shifting banks of mud and sand that are exposed at high tide are certainly part of the river delta. The influence of the Dee stretches well out into the ocean - as it is now easy to tell by the forest of offshore wind farms that have taken advantage of shallow water offshore. Looking at the map the end to the river seemed a lot clearer to me than it was on the ground. A reasonable place to declare that it has reached the end would be next to the Shotten Steel works, just down the road from the paper factory and where the A548 heads past the power station.

That is not exactly the most romantic of ends for one of the finest rivers in the country. I turned off to try and find it at a place called Garden City near Connah's Quay. Anyone might be forgiven for assuming that a place called garden city was in a city and in a delightfully green setting. It conjures up images of suburban streets where people mow lawns before heading off for their job as an investment banker. This one is stuck between a busy dual carriageway and an industrial estate. It was originally planned to provide high quality homes to attract people to come and work in the nearby steelworks. Driving through you could tell that someone had made a serious attempt to build an estate of pleasant housing. You could also tell that the project had not been entirely a success. It now had the feel of a place that had been cut off and neglected. I parked just off the estate, as close as I could to the river, and walked a couple of hundred yards across flat washed out farmland to reach the banks. There wasn't much to see. Just straight featureless banks of what had been turned into a ship canal. In one direction the main thing to see was an iron bridge leading into the steelworks. In the other it was a line of pylons. Between its straightened banks the river wasn't exactly doing a lot to demonstrate some last signs of life and energy. It was flowing backwards with the tide. Taking with it a few pieces of floating plastic and timber that most likely would be taken back out to sea with the next tide. To clutter up somewhere else.

I passed up on the opportunity to walk down the river bank to explore the path to the steelworks. It seemed a long trudge for little reward so I went back to the car and drove there instead. A succession of roundabouts and dual carriageway took me past the industrial estate on one side to the mouth of the river. The land around here is flat and cheap. The transport connection are good. And there is a long history of industry going right back to Roman times. Local people need the jobs in these factories and the country needs the income from them and the products they produce. So it is not entirely a tragedy that the mouth of the Dee has become an industrial heartland. Industry has to go somewhere and the battle around here is not to get rid of the industry in order to create a charming wilderness for wildlife. The battle is to keep enough of it going whilst doing as little harm as possible. Ask almost any local and they will tell you that they want to keep the Tata steelworks alive and functioning and that they want to see further investment and modernisation to keep it competitive. They might also tell you that it doesn't make for the prettiest of views and that the waters around here haven't always been the cleanest. The local flatfish have a nasty tendency to come with added ulceration and the gangs of cockle pickers working out in the bay may not have informed their buyers that their shellfish will have been filtering the highest levels of PCBs, Dieldrin and Mercury of any estuary in Britain.[32] The local industries are doing their best to clean up their act but there are still major chemical works on the banks of the nearby Mersey and it takes time to transform an environment that has been subject to heavy damage. Efforts to offset their activities and to do business with a little less impact on the environment were clear to see as I turned the car around and headed up river towards some rather nicer parts of the Dee. Giant sections of the fields on the left hand side of the dual carriageway had been covered with solar panels. It must have stretched for over a mile in length and been four hundred metres wide and generated significant amounts of power for the industrial estate. It didn't do much for the view.

If you want a good view and a beautiful stretch of river then you can't do much better than Chester so I headed there. The modern Dee seems to change instantly from a dour industrial waterway into a charming river as soon as it hits the city and reaches the end of its tidal stretches. I parked the car below the castle walls and began to walk along the banks. Above me was a dramatic wall of red sandstone building blocks supporting defensive structures. It loomed high and proud representing hour after hour of backbreaking work for medieval stone masons. Each individual block had weathered to a different extent. Centuries of wind, rain and frost had worked away at the rock picking away the ancient layers of sand at varied speeds. However hard the pressure of gravity had pressed down on the red sands of the desert that had once covered this landscape it had not been enough to make the rock strong enough to last hundreds of years without showing serious signs of wear. Now the different shades of red and the variety of the rounded shapes that had resulted made every detail of the giant stone structure interesting to examine. Time and red sandstone are a good combination.

---

[32] Mike Griffiths, The History of the River Dee, (Gwasg Carreg Gwalch, 2000) p168

The builders hadn't had to go far to get the rock. Looking across the river it was easy to spot places where it poked upwards through the river silt to create natural outcrops. Chester wasn't just a good place to build because it was at the limit of tidal navigation and therefore of easy transport. It was a good place to build because it had solid rock foundations in an area of low lying land that floods easily. This has made it a popular choice of location to live and work in since the earliest times. Here you could create good defensive structures and if conditions were right you could even ford the river. Given the amount of trade that wanted to pass over the Dee at this convenient crossing point and the difficulty of relying on capricious river conditions, Chester also got a bridge over the river at a very early date. There has been a bridge here off and on since Roman times and the Old Dee Bridge that is there at the moment has been standing strong since a rebuilding in 1367. The road running over it goes straight under the city walls and heads off towards the depths of Wales. I stood on top of those walls and got a real feel of what it must have been like to be a Roman soldier staring out from the defences and wondering exactly when and where the next rebellion of cross Welsh highlanders was brewing.

Walking a little further upriver I found that the tide had now reached its limits. Just up river from the bridge there was a section of slight turbulence. Below it the river was still running backwards from the sea. Above it the Dee was running slowly downwards towards that same sea. The two forces were gently meeting each other and cancelling out. Underneath was the weir that normally marks the borderline between fresh water and bracken. I had been fortunate to catch the river at exactly the right moment to see the weir covered up and the Dee full to the brim.

Above where the weir can normally be seen the river attracts the most tourists of anywhere along its route. Coach loads of weekenders come here to take a short ride upriver on one of the flat bottomed tourist crafts that ease you upstream to the sound of a commentary that has been delivered many times before. You can ride on the Lady Dianna in comfort as you slide past the Georgian houses and the parks that line the banks and be confident that fellow tourists have been doing this for many decades. The Victorians made much the same journey but they decided to build themselves a nice little wrought iron bandstand to add to the fun provided by a day out on the river. I pictured them enjoying a bit of wholesome musical entertainment whilst strolling along the banks in their Sunday best.

Those Victorians had also laid out a very attractive park on the high land just past the tourist boats. I decided not to walk over the tempting old footbridge and then follow 'Lady Dianna' upstream but instead to climb to the top of a high river cut cliff and enjoy the views from up there. It proved a good choice. Grosvenor Park led me through interesting walkways, past grand old trees to a viewing platform that enabled me to see the sweep of the Dee curving around perfectly shaped upriver bends. Above Chester the Dee becomes a geography teacher's joy as it performs a series of endlessly changing meanders across low land dividing Wales from Cheshire. The land it crosses is so flat that it has been under the sea in recent geological history. Looking out from the last of the high banks on the edge of the city enables you to see some of the first and the largest of these meanders as the river struggles to find any consistent direction amongst a land formed mainly from its own mud and silt.

I turned back towards the city keeping to the high ground just alongside the river. This is a place of very ancient settlement. There are ruins of an old church, well preserved medieval walls and a Roman amphitheatre. It has been used for a roundabout. Seating for spectators watching a Roman prize fight tends to be in a graceful curve so that everyone had a good view of the action as the criminals got executed, the beasts got ripped apart and they tried hard to put on a good show without losing too many of the expensively trained gladiators. At some time in Chester's modern history some bright spark had decided that the curve made by the amphitheatre was also an ideal shape for the inner ring road. So the first thing I spotted as I approached some of the most important Roman remains in the country was a long line of primary school children carrying plastic shields being ferried safely across a busy road. Those young kids were going to need powerful imaginations to ignore the traffic and conjure up images of Romans watching slaves fight for their lives. I have to be honest that my own imaginative ability began to suffer a fraction when I discovered that half of the stadium is framed by the road whilst the other half is firmly beneath a badly degenerating building from the 18th century called Dee House.

As grade 2 listed buildings go Dee House must be amongst the ugliest. Plans to turn it into a visitor centre hit problems as soon as anyone looked seriously into the cost of transforming a neglected former girls school into something that might do credit to the impressive Roman remains its borders on and covers up.[33] Instead the place is currently being used by the local council to store building materials. From the floor of the Roman amphitheatre you can look up and see the boarded up windows, the bushes growing out of the walls and the unattractive red brick facade. Approaching more closely a small sign informed me that archaeologists had performed test digs under the former convent and found that there was very little of the Roman ruins left undamaged. I was left with the uncharitable thought that however meagre they might be then it would be better to get rid of the listed monstrosity and expose the other half of an amphitheatre so impressive that it once housed 8,000 spectators.

---

[33] Chester Chronicle, 7th Aug 2014.

Fortunately the high land immediately above the river doesn't just contain disrespected Roman remains. It also contains the earliest Cathedral in the city. Indeed one of the most important places of worship in early Britain. The church of St John the Baptist doesn't get many visitors as most tour groups head for the huge Cathedral in the centre of town. Personally I have to confess that I mainly walked in to get away from a brief shower of rain. It wasn't long before I realised my good fortune. This was no ordinary Parish Church. Giant columns stretch up to a great height using nothing but their sheer bulk to support the structures above, yet still managing to look graceful thanks to their rounded shapes.

This way of building is exactly what the Normans liked to use when they first got round to demonstrating their construction skills to the locals. You only have to look at the size of this former cathedral and the quality of the work and then compare it to the small buildings that have survived from what went before to realise why those Normans won so many battles. Technologically they were clearly far ahead of anything people from around here had seen before. It didn't take the Normans long to work out that they could deliver that message loudly and clearly by demonstrating enough control and confidence to put up religious buildings that made a real statement. Only nine years after the invasion a decision was made to move Bishop Peter De Leya's base from Litchfield to Chester. He immediately set about building a brand new cathedral on this fantastic site overlooking the river plain. Anyone from Wales thinking of launching an attack would only need to glance at it rising high above an already impressive sandstone ridge and they would instantly know that it wouldn't be a great idea to mess with the Normans. Or at least not in one of their solid bases like Chester.

What is left now is an astonishingly soaring structure. Sit inside and look up to the roof way above you and you see rows of perfectly proportioned arches marking out each stage of the building's climb to the heights. I was dwarfed by the scale. Yet on going outside I quickly realised that what was left was only a shadow of what had once been constructed. Beyond the back wall there are a set of red sandstone ruins which are the remains of the rest of the former Cathedral. The tower here only collapsed in 1881 but the neglect had been going on for a very long time. Over the centuries different decision makers kept forming new views about what was the best place for a Cathedral and St John's suffered from the bureaucratic changes. First it was decided to make Coventry the Cathedral city for this part of the land instead of Chester. So the status of being a Cathedral was lost. Then in the time of Henry VIII it was decided that Chester did actually need a Cathedral - but not this one. They picked a different site closer to the centre of town. The new Cathedral - the one that currently attracts so many tourists - steadily began to overshadow the old fashioned one on the river bank. The final blow appears to have come when Elizabeth the First decided to be kind enough to allow the locals to keep parts of St John's as a parish church. Provided they let her have the lead off the roof! That couldn't have been easy to do when they were dealing with a building of this stature and could only get up there on wooden scaffolding. Somehow they complied with the royal request to take away the valuable lead and still managed to preserve the fabric of around half of the building. Outside, and exposed to the wind and the rain coming in off the Atlantic, any part of the giant complex of buildings that was too big for the parishioners' needs was simply left to crumble.[34]

Which is a shame as St John's claims to be the site of one of the most important events in early British history and also the culmination of one of the most important river trips ever undertaken in the country. It is said to be the place where King

---

[34] For the history of the church I used Gordon Emery's publications: The Chester Guide, (Masons, 2002) and Curious Chester (Zanders, 1999) along with the St John's Church guidebooklet

Edgar received homage from the other less significant kings of Britain and brought unity and peace to the English nation. Which is not a bad achievement for someone that most of us have never even heard of. Like many people I can't claim to be very well up on the history of England between the Romans leaving and the Normans arriving. I had managed to pick up that King Alfred got driven into the swamplands and was so distracted by the experience that he burnt some cakes. And then he fought his way back to create a powerful Saxon kingdom. I had succeeded in tracing bits of King Offa's huge dike and knew that it stretched 120 miles along the border with Wales before finishing strategically close to Chester. I didn't know the first thing about King Edgar.

It turns out that he was every bit as significant to our history as either Alfred or Offa and went through a set of experiences every bit as colourful. Like most Kings, Edgar acquired a nick name. He is was known as the peaceable. Which is quite an achievement for a man who has been accused of marrying his step parents' daughter only to divorce her when he got bored, forcing a nun into his bed against her consent, and then murdering a man so that he could marry his good looking wife. Apparently that last action prevents bigamy![35] If there is even the remotest truth to these accusations then he was in serious need of a good publicity machine to polish up his image. Edgar had the best one going. He was the church candidate. In particular he was the Benedictine monks' candidate. Since they were the busiest historians of the time it may not be entirely surprising that it is mainly their version of the truth that has come down to us. In their work there isn't a lot about any indiscretions that he may actually have committed. The good monks tended to record his time in office as a model period during which there were few battles but many sensible

---

[35] Barbara Yorke makes it clear that the sources for these accusations are not neutral and there is much doubt about his actual behaviour. See Edgar, King of the English, Ed Donald Scragg (Boydell Press, 2008) p144-157

reforms. Which is probably why most of us know so little about him. Quiet strong government doesn't make for colourful history. He managed to combine huge swathes of territory into one English nation step by steady step. He appears to have been very good at diplomacy and at being in the right place at the right time. It is also a fair bet that he had a strong enough army to mean that he could command allegiance without actually having to fight too often. Some kings before him had tried to combine the early kingdoms of Mercia and Wessex. Edgar succeeded not only in doing this securely but also in including the huge Kingdom of Northumbria and he did it without major bloodshed. When a number of minor kings from more remote areas decided it was wise to pay him some homage he became the first person since the Romans who felt able to plausibly claim that they were the ruler of Britain.

To cement the achievement he is said to have invited 8 British kings to join him in Chester to recognise his overall power. They all took a boat trip together on the Dee making the journey along this bit of the river a contender for the earliest tourist ride in British history. In 987 a bunch of aristocrats had a lovely day out on the river in Chester, feasted and celebrated grandly, and then pulled over to the banks and headed into a nearby church. There Edgar was formally recognised as the overall King of the whole country using ceremonies that are still copied in the British coronation service to this day. The guidebook to St John's church informed me that this took place in the Saxon church that stood on the site of the fine building I'd entered to get out of the rain. It conjured up wonderful images of royalty in all their regalia working their way up the same hill that I had just climbed and then participating in a suitably solemn church ceremony exactly where I stood. Unfortunately the best academic study I could find suggests that the events probably took place at a different Church in Chester called St Werburg's.[36] I would have much preferred to have believed the other version of events. Edgar deserves to be better known for his achievements and the current church of St John's is a wonderfully atmospheric place to stand and visualise heroic events through a suitably romantic haze.

The image I was left with of the river at Chester was one of great continuity. Tourists have been enjoying themselves on this section of the river for over 1200 years and I could see why. It is a thoroughly relaxed and enjoyable place to spend time. I headed up river hoping to find equally interesting but less well trodden sites. For the first twenty or so miles I was travelling over flat land where the river passes through a succession of small villages each of which seems to be competing to have the prettiest ancient bridge and the finest church. Bangor on Dee won the contest for me with a crumbling red sandstone bridge and a charming church displaying pictures of a dreadful flood which had inundated the whole area. The land here is too flat and wide to provide much protection when the river has to cope with weeks of heavy Welsh rain. Over the centuries thick deposits of mud have been lain down and turned into fertile agricultural land. Back in the days when farming was the dominant activity this was no bad thing. Rich soil supported rich landowners and communities large and vibrant enough to build large churches and equally impressive bridges.

Then suddenly the meandering river and the wide plain comes to an end. The Welsh hills start to close in on it and squeeze the river. It begins to take on a very different character. Below those hills the river's slow ramble across its own deposits doesn't make for a landscape packed with dramatic features. It is only when the high ground starts to rear up in the distance that the Dee starts to really get into its stride as one of the prettiest rivers in the country. Or rather the Afron Dyfrdwy does. It becomes a Welsh river. Down on the plains for long

---

[36] Ibid, C.P. Lewis, p121

stretches the Dee is the only feature of the landscape that is clear enough to be used as a demarcation border and so England and Wales are often separated in mid stream. There is doubting the nationality of the river once you enter the hills and mountains. It now becomes proudly and firmly Welsh.

Between the flat lowland plains and the mountains there is a sequence of river that has cut its way deep into the hills. It winds its way from side to side of the valley pushing hard against the hills on one side and then another. The land above has been washed smooth by geological eras of rainfall but all that water enables the river to cut more steeply into the valley sides the further upstream you move. The result is that most transport uses the valley bottom and then struggles to cope with the twists and turns of the river. At some point almost all routes have to switch from one side of the waterway to the other to avoid being squeezed up the hillside where the Dee presses hard against it. This has proved a hard enough task for road engineers but they have managed it with a series of steep roads crossing bridges from many different eras. For the early canal builders things weren't quite so easy. You can't put hills into canals and every lock wastes a lot of time and energy and makes the enterprise uneconomic. The best way of both ensuring a reliable supply of water for the canal and taking it close to coal mines that were significant customers was to move the whole canal across the river valley on an aqueduct. The result is a marvel of engineering which deservedly gets world heritage status. Eighteen graceful arches rise up 38 metres above the river and have been carrying canal boats safely across for more than 200 years.

I parked the car near the canal just above the village of Pontcysyllte and set off expecting a challenging walk would be needed to get to the viaduct. It was a lot easier than I had thought. There was a canal basin right next to the car park and within a hundred yards it led you to the start of the dramatic crossing. The Pontcysyllte viaduct is a strange sight. I don't know if it is to do with the height of the structure or the fact that it stretches out straight before you for over 300 metres but it seems much too narrow to contain a boat. Even a canal boat. It looked to me like someone had decided to elongate a bath for a very great distance. By contrast the walkway alongside the thin tank of murky water was considerably more generous than I had feared. It was possible to stride along the bank feeling safe and secure using a path that had been constructed for horses and had a cast iron railing that had been built solidly enough to hold one in check if it decided to panic. The occupants of the first canal boat that came across showed a distinct preference for standing on this towpath side of the boat. I couldn't say I blamed them. On the other side the boat stood high and proud above the water with a drop down to the Dee that must be the equivalent of a 15 storey building.

This is just about the most intimidating height you can have. Go much higher and it is possible to lose awareness of the reality of the drop as the features in the landscape become too small and distant. Stuck on the outside of a canal boat on a windy day, supported only by arches and ironwork put up a couple of hundred years ago, it is all too possible to imagine what it would be like to fall over the side and straight down to the Dee. Any passenger brave enough to stand there is well above any protective parapet and must feel incredibly vulnerable. The boat floats high enough in the water. Then there is your own height to add to the experience. The lateral movement of the barge across the drop makes it worse. I quickly came to the conclusion that this was the kind of canal boat excursion that you don't attempt unless you are very confident of your skills and your head for heights.

I walked slowly across the aqueduct taking in the changing view. Downriver you can see another spectacular set of arches crossing the river where the railway engineers had also found themselves faced with little choice other than to spend a lot of time and effort bridging the river. The Cefn Mawr viaduct uses only a paltry ten arches to cross the river and is only a little over 150 years old but still looks sufficiently spectacular from a distance to be frequently mistaken for the more famous canal aqueduct. It draws the eye away from a landscape that has been damaged by centuries of industrial activity. Unfortunately it can't do the same job for the nose. Just after the canal crosses the river the local water company has decided that a bit of flat land next to the Dee is an ideal place to put a small sewage farm. There can't be too many world heritage sites that have been selected by the authorities as the location for their water waste management programmes. Warm fetid air has a tendency to rise up and to carry with it sufficient aromatic particles to ensure that even the most insensitive human olifactory tract has little difficulty in identifying the smell. I got the full benefit just after crossing the highest point.

Up river from the viaduct the air gets a lot fresher as the wind blows in from the mountains. The Dee starts to slide across a succession of small rapids beneath imposing hillsides. After leaving the Pontcysyllte viaduct I headed for Llangollen where the scenery has been picturesque enough to attract outsiders for a very long time. Many of them come for the Eisteddfod. Others for a glorious ride on the heritage railway or to follow the canal further up into the hills. I came to visit the home of two women who were serious celebrities in their day but have been somewhat forgotten since.

I stayed in a hotel called the Hand which had been around long enough to develop serious eccentricities. It is the kind of place where you find an ancient keyboard instrument of dubious quality left on a stair well as a feature. At some point someone had decided that this was a thing of charm and beauty which deserved to be put on display but it now felt like it had been neglected there for so long that no one could be bothered to move it or dust it. My room was stuck in the eaves and had a crack in the sink. It was, nevertheless, clear that the Hand had once been a very grand establishment indeed. It had high ceilings, plenty of good solid wood and great wide staircases leading into hidden depths. Yet its main attraction was the outside garden. The Hand occupies one of the prime bits of real estate on the banks of the Dee. You can sit and enjoy your meal watching the river flow over rounded blocks of stone as you soak up the last rays of the evening sun. By the time it reaches Llangollen the Dee has gained a bit of speed and energy so that it swirls and bubbles a little whenever it passes over a section of slightly harder bedrock. Down here below the pub the river was just deep enough on this particular day to provide a couple of feet of cover across perhaps ten yards of constantly varying movement. There was a low evening light giving a dark glassy colour to the deeper sections and the odd duck paddling about on them. It was all very enjoyable.

The reason for the rather fine riverside garden is that back in time the Hand had once been so posh that it was the only place in town where anyone of note would think of staying. It had its own carriages and used them to pick up the regular stream of grand visitors who wished to come and see the famous Ladies of Llangollen. These were the women that I had come to find out more about and they acquired their fame the hard way. Back in the 1770s it didn't do to be a woman of intelligence – especially if you lacked access to your own financial resources. As Jane Austin has taught us all so well the best you could hope for if you hung around in your relatives' homes for too long was to be patronised and occasionally humiliated in order to remind you that you really should have been married off well before now. The worst that could happen was that you found yourself dependent on the hospitality of a man who thought that providing a home for a distant relative also provided a first class opportunity to make unwanted advances. Especially if his wife was somewhat tired of providing sexual services and was quite happy to nudge you in the direction of the elderly male of the house. That was the situation which young Sarah Ponsonby found herself trapped in and she didn't like being stuck in a remote corner of Ireland fending off a vain elderly man one little bit. Down the road from her was a close older friend who was having an almost equally hard time over pressure that she should enter a convent because she was 39 and a bit of a useless expense.[37] The solution they arrived at was to run away together and set up home in a remote valley in Wales. It took them two goes, a major scandal and a lot of arguments with their relatives but eventually they managed escape and to get their families to agree that the least shameful option was to make the women a small annual payment to be rid of them both in the wilds of Wales.

The two women set about creating a better life for themselves with real determination. They decided that they would embrace their isolation and use it to live the life of intellectual pursuits. To their minds the best way to express their considerable learning was to create a perfect home in a perfect landscape. Back then that meant the picturesque. Llangollen does picturesque with ease. So the ladies took on a small home high up above the river valley where they could sit outside of an evening reading uplifting literature. As they did so they could look down over the steep sides of a delightful little stream or upwards across the Dee to see the ruins of Castle Dinas Bran standing proudly on the opposite hilltop. During the day they spent their time planning and making improvements to their new home. Gradually they built it up to become a near self-sufficient model farm from which they could sell enough produce to help meet some very pressing bills. The house itself they developed and kitted out in their own particular style, covering the main interior walls with the most amazing collection of carved wooden panels. Despite constantly struggling with money they spent lavishly on an impressive collection of books and spent their evenings

---

[37] Elizabeth Mavor, The Ladies of Llangollen, p24

discussing the best French literature or the latest ideas of the romantic movement. With astonishing consistency of purpose they turned their lives into a powerful expression of the ideals of that philosophy. A home away from it all in dramatic scenery where two people were seeking to develop their minds, express their artistic sensibilities and develop a small patch of the land into a productive but beautiful expression of their thoughts. What could be more attractive to aficionados of the romantic cause who had spent too much time in the big city? Either then or now. As a result their fame amongst fellow enthusiasts began to spread.

People gradually began to make the journey to find out what the ideals they shared with these women looked like in action and came back sufficiently filled with enthusiasm to persuade others to follow in their footsteps. After a long hard period of social isolation the ladies began to find their situation had utterly transformed. They could now scarcely get a moment of peace to themselves and the Hand Hotel was doing a roaring trade in hiring out its carriages and renting out its finest rooms. Wordsworth came, as did the Duke of Gloucester.[38] On one day in 1821 they received visits from 22 people including 7 Lords and 4 Ladies with the visits commencing in the morning and continuing right up until supper, after which Lord and Lady Ormonde stayed the night[39]. All of this in the age before railways when travelling was serious business. Personally I thought it wise to avoid asking the hotel reception to order me their finest carriage and so I walked the steep hill up from my hotel following in their footsteps only to find that the house no longer attracts too many of the great and good or even the mildly curious. The climb is enough to put off a lot of tourists and the difficulty of parking most of the rest. So I had the house to myself.

---

[38] Ibid p198
[39] Ibid p183

A very pleasant tea room had been created in the grounds where I sprang quite a surprise on the staff by asking for a ticket to view the house instead of just going for the coffee and cake like the rest of their customers. Out in front of the house there have been a lot of changes since the ladies lived there and you now approach via a well-manicured lawn and some neatly arranged flower beds. Round the back there is rather more of the landscape they created. Hidden away at the end of the charming rear garden you can find the little bower the women constructed where they liked to read and chat of an evening. Below it they designed a winding path to take them down a steep slope and across the little stream that had cut it. It is still there so I followed the route of their favourite nightly stroll and found myself in the depths of the ravine surrounded by giant beech trees that were stretching straight up towards the light. A short way up the valley a small wooden bridge led to a second path which led them, and me, back to the house and completed a very pleasant short circuit.

At the door of the house the same person who was running the café was doubling up as ticket collector. I was ushered in and offered some helpful tips on what there was to see. The wooden panelling that the ladies spent so long trying to put in is still there. Hours upon hours of work have gone into carving every conceivable pattern into each small rectangle and then even more hours have gone into polishing the dark wood into a deep luscious shine. It looks as if no single surface has been left undecorated and no two decorations have ever been repeated. The entire staircase leading you upstairs into the house has been carved with real skill at a time when craft workers had the time, the patience and the training to do the work well. Two other things struck me powerfully. One was the library where it was possible to get a real feel for the breadth and the depths of the women's learning. These ladies weren't playing at being intellectuals. They were reading heavy texts in several different languages and corresponding with the best and the brightest of their age. The other was their bedroom.

It is easy to stand here and imagine the nocturn activities of two women who shared the same bed for decades in an age when female sexuality was suspect. It would be nice to think that women this long ago not only had the courage to break free from genuine patriarchal control but went on to express their right to enjoy physical love with whoever they chose regardless of gender. It is, however, impossible to know what went on in their bedroom because they never told anyone. They reacted badly to a press article that hinted at a physical relationship so it is entirely possible that they simply weren't interested in one. It is also very plausible to believe that they were. Speculation on which it was rather misses the point. Instead I think it is important to focus on the fact that a couple of hundred years ago two women voiced their love for each other very clearly and openly and asserted their right to live together in a romantic attachment without any desire for male physical affection. They paid a very high price for that financially and socially especially at first. But gradually their decision to live by their own rules began to draw increasing numbers of admirers. Their determination to make their own choices turned them into well-known characters that were admired and respected. Having been condemned to live outside of polite society in a quiet backwater it must have been a spectacularly fine thing to live long enough in their own way to find that society started beating a path to their door and they became a tourist attraction in their own right.

I chatted away for a while with the man who had shown me in. Apparently the ladies home had gained a licence to conduct weddings and was doing occasional trade as a venue for same sex weddings between women. I could well see why. Bravery in their own choices had paid off against the odds and it felt nice to think that women a couple of centuries on wanted to thank them for this enough to make their own commitments at their former home.

The next day I got back into my car and headed further up the Dee towards its headwaters. I picked the perfect day for it. Late autumn with a mixture of sun and rain created a magical selection of colours. The road runs mostly upwards following the river, curving away from it to find an easy route and then finding itself drawn back towards the valley bottom. This made for interesting driving as I was never far from a rising curve in the road that needs its fair share of concentration. But there are also little sections where I could relax enough to glance across the valley and see the leaves on the trees taking on different colours. Scientifically the cause of the variety in the leaves is simply that nutrients are being sucked back deeper into the living core leaving only unwanted tannins of different shades. Rarely can one creature's efforts to rid itself of poison have worked better to provide accidental pleasure for another. The selection of yellows, golds, browns and reds was different for each species, different for each locality's microclimate and different even for each leaf on every branch of the same tree. In many places the road is fringed by mature trees and even driving carefully it was easy to get a good view of them lining the road with all this variety. In other spots the views were more open and it became possible to look out across the Dee into the distance. It had become a river that worked its way across a wide valley with hills that gradually get stronger with each broad meander. Millions of years of flowing water have gentled out the landscape so that the valley sides are beginning to gain some respectable heights but are always rounded off. At one point I looked down across all the subtle colours to see a sharply focused rainbow seeming to run down into the depths of the valley lighting up a landscape of open fields dappled with small groves of different kinds of trees. Then the sunlight that illuminated the rainbow so precisely disappeared and within seconds rain was pouring

176

down and I could barely see the road in front of me. When it rains in this part of Wales it can do so with all the benefit of the full length of the Atlantic blowing behind it. It did exactly that.

I followed what I could still see of the road as far as Bala, in order to explore the lake which is pretty much the real source of the Dee. Lake Bala is the largest natural lake in Wales and water from a whole series of streams comes down from the hills above to fill it. Deciding which of those streams is the actual start point of the Dee isn't a very worthwhile exercise. It is the collective power of all the rain falling on all of those hills and sliding down towards the Lake which provides the real energy for the river. By the time the storm had abated and I got to walk out to the edge of the water it was late in the day. The great masses of moving air that had brought in such great quantities of rain were still moving but by now they were only driving small little remnant clouds forward. Some were black and angry with jagged little edges beneath them where sheets of water were collapsing down towards the ground, but most were various shades of white and grey. The moving mass of air and moisture formed a wonderfully fluid and mobile background for the scene across the water. Lake Bala covers land that has been flattened out by some ancient glacier. So the floor or the valley needs a bit of drama to set it off. It was getting that in full measure. Different lines of hills rose up above the lake each one fainter and more remote than the last. Close by the slopes were quite gentle and rolling and it was easy to spot a variety of trees and farmhouses clinging to the sides and giving them colour. Beyond those first low hills there was another range where you could just make out a little of the colour and none of the detail as they rose up to provide a second and a third horizon. Then there was a row of higher hills that were fainter and looked even more dramatic. All that could be made out below their distant skylines were the bare shapes of a grey mass. Finally, right at the back there was a thin pencil line of the high mountain landscape that could easily have been mistaken for cloud.

I stood for a long while watching the light fade, the clouds move and the ripples travel across the surface of the lake. No part of the lake was quite the same colour as any other. The simple pressure of air on water produced such random variation that every tiny one-inch high wave got hit by the light at a slightly different angle and either swallowed some of the approaching darkness or shone back as silver, white, grey or some new mixture of all three. A few sections of water were still and glassy. Others had been colonised by a small group of birds who had done their work for the day and looked like they were settling down for the night. At the edge of the water a single pied wagtail scudded across the surface trying to catch a late flying insect. Then it sat on a rock and used its tail to illustrate how it got the name. Finally it decided there might still be some good eating still to be had and flew on a bit further. I also decided it was time to move on before it got too dark.

I walked round the lake looking for the place where the Dee emerges from it and sets off down towards Chester and the sea. I kept stopping to look back at the latest angle that the lake and the hills were forming against the declining light and the clouds. It made for slow progress but the light kept changing and every new perspective seemed to improve on the view. When I eventually got to the river I was surprised to see the size of it. I had expected to discover a much-diminished flow and something a little bigger than a stream but not yet really a river. Instead the Dee looked bigger than it had done miles further downstream. It was almost immediately joined by another strong flow of water coming down from the hills turning it into a substantial current. Even allowing for the rain and the rise in the river this upper section seemed to be flowing wider and stronger than I'd seen it lower down. This made no sense. How can a river be bigger upstream than it is down? Then I remembered just how much this river has been messed with and managed. When the river gets further downstream a great deal of it gets stolen.

That theft of water has been happening for a long time. Over two hundred years ago Thomas Telford syphoned off large amounts to ensure that his canal had a reliable supply without taking too much notice of the impact on local fishery. Back in the 1950s the civic officials from the Liverpool corporation did much the same in order to provide their residents with water. Then they decided that it would be good for them if they could pull a more reliable supply of water out of the Dee than was possible with a river that rose and fell every time rain hit the mountains. So they decided to create a dam across the Afon Trywery to regulate the flow of it down towards Bala and beyond. It did its job and flooded the valley to a depth of over 40 metres, creating a lake a mile long. Unfortunately it also flooded the local village. Despite every MP in Wales being opposed to the scheme it was forced through Parliament and the Welsh speaking villagers were kicked off their land and out of their community for the convenience of an English city. It doesn't take a lot of imagination to figure out how that went down with the locals.

The next morning I headed upwards to look for the signs of the flooded valley and to explore the source of the Dee. The route was so quiet and so free from air pollution that in places it was possible to see tiny little clumps of white green moss growing on the tips of the few deciduous trees that had survived the attention of past woodcutters. Most of the landscape on these hills above Bala has been cleared for sheep and people have tried to ruin some of the rest by creating dark plantations of boring conifers. But it is still spectacular countryside. Out here above the far edge of a delightful lake I came across a small area of low shrubby trees that seemed to have escaped the hand of humans for a very long time. These weren't straight growing giants but small strong trees that kept close to the ground to avoid the worst of the weather. Great gnarled stumps of bulbous material had built up around the base of the trunks in what looked like an attempt to thicken them sufficiently to withstand the wind. Blotches of lichens clung to the ridges and furrows colouring parts of the bark grey and others green. The highest branches had already lost every one of their leaves and were standing out stark and black. They looked like a remnant of a primeval forest sitting undisturbed in a place where they had belonged for centuries. Then something caught my eye behind them. There was a disused railway embankment running down towards the village that Liverpool Corporation had flooded. The line had closed when the village it served went under the water. This wasn't a natural lake. It was the one that had been engineered and altered for the convenience of city dwellers many miles away. Even up here at the remotest headwaters of the Dee the river and the landscape had been managed and controlled.

The Dee is only half the river it was. The great quantities of rain that fall on these Welsh mountains naturally creates a very powerful river that rises and falls spectacularly according to what is happening way out in the Atlantic. Instead of still owning the full force of every drop of water than falls in its huge catchment area the river now has to cope with the share that we allow it to take. Like most rivers in the modern world it has been managed and controlled from its start to its finish by human actions. Yet even an abandoned railway line running towards a village drowned for the convenience of others cannot quite undo the fact that this is still countryside that wants to be wild. And it can be spectacularly impressive. Despite all our efforts to mess with it the Dee remains one of the most beautiful rivers in the country.

What must it have been like before?

The Dee - Scotland

At first sight the Dee that runs from the Scottish Highlands down to reach the sea at Aberdeen looks to be a wilder river in a more natural landscape than the Welsh and English version. It gathers its strength from some of the most dramatic and isolated mountains in the whole of the British Isles. You don't have to go far from the top of the Grampians to find powerful streams trying desperately to take all of the water that falls on this side of the highlands rapidly away downstream. It looks like the upland channels have been cut through an unmanaged and unchanging landscape where deer, grouse and sheep roam free. The kind of place for an invigorating hill walk across open countryside or through deep forests where signs of human activity are few and far between. Right from its very beginning the river tempts you to spend an afternoon on a spot of salmon fishing in clear unspoiled waters or to strike out on your own across nature in the raw. Surely here, if anywhere, you can get away from the bustle and noise of people and spend time in properly unspoiled countryside. Nothing could be more different from the heavily managed and manicured land that you find in the rest of the UK than this pristine wilderness.

Except of course that it isn't pristine. The land hereabout has been subject to every bit as much change and manipulation as that surrounding the Welsh Dee or the Yorkshire uplands. Much of this area was home to subsistence farming until quite recent history. The highlands of Scotland can provide that wonderful feeling of being free from the constant pressure of humanity crowding in around you for a very simple reason. Most of the local residents were cleared off the land when they became economically inconvenient. The unfortunate Welsh villagers above Bala lost their homes near the summit of their river Dee to quite recent decisions made by water engineers that they had never met who were working in an office a long way away. Many of the Scottish crofters lost them much earlier to individual landowners that they knew personally but who had found a more profitable way of using the land than collecting a few scraps of rent money from people who could barely get by. In most of the Scottish-Highlands that meant introducing sheep instead of people. In the majority of the glens that feed the Dee it was more frivolous than that. The old established crofting communities were cleared away to provide recreational hunting of deer and grouse. A fashion for shooting is the prime force shaping great chunks of the countryside management around Braemar.

On a sunny day in summer you can easily understand the attraction of being out and about in such rugged landscape. This is countryside with strong features and ideal for a morning of healthy outdoor recreation. Standing up to your knees in cold water, trying to catch a salmon, is a peaceful relaxing activity on a nice day when you've got the right equipment. It is therefore not hard to see why anyone with enough money might be very easily tempted to purchase an estate up here in order to enjoy the pleasures of the open air whenever they felt the need for a break from the pressures of city life. A long warm summer day, the company of like-minded friends, plenty of exercise followed by a hearty meal and a nice warm fire are exactly what the doctor ordered. In a howling gale in the middle of winter life in the heart of the Scottish Highlands has always been rather harder. Particularly if you had to try and grow enough food to keep your family alive. Even the valleys around here can be intimidating places in the wrong weather. The communities that lived on this land before the highland clearances didn't have much choice about whether they went out to look after their cattle or their crops on a cold wet day in winter and certainly didn't have access to high quality breathable fabrics which are light to wear and shed water with ease. It must have been a constant struggle to survive in this environment. The winters are hard and long and the summers are unreliable. It only takes too much rain or too little of it and even the toughest of crops can fail. Back in the 18th century if you were farming this far from civilisation you couldn't simply ship in replacement food quickly and easily when things went wrong. Getting wagons and supplies over the passes wasn't easy. More importantly the money simply wasn't there for the vast majority of subsistence crofters to buy anything they became short of. It just wasn't possible to make enough money in good years to get by in bad.

Famine struck in the Highlands of Scotland in 1680, 1688, the 1690s, 1740-41, 1751, 1756, 1772-3 and 1782.[40] That is a horrible regularity to fail to feed your kids. The intimidating landscape, the weather and the constant anxiety of living on the edge made this a tough marginal existence. Landlords began to realise that starving subsistence farmers don't generate much rental income whereas sheep can live in some of the harshest of places, provide lots of valuable raw material to sell to the Yorkshire woollen mills and produce some very good meat. Yet most of the Highlanders weren't cleared away by a violent set piece eviction. The majority were eased off their land by a slower process of attrition that was every bit as relentless but a lot easier to enforce. Tenancies weren't renewed when they ran out resulting in families leaving one by one and a steady loss of strength in the community. The old often remained in the area but many of the younger people adopted a very different lifestyle in the growing industrial cities like Glasgow instead of battling it out to scratch a living off the land. Many headed even further afield and ended up in the States. Gradually the land was hollowed out of both the energetic young people and the ability to resist change and maintain a rich tradition.

This means that, as with most history, the nature of the Highland clearances is hotly disputed. Was it a case of evil landlords and their agents destroying long-lasting communities where people had learned all the skills they

---

[40] Eric Richards, The Highland Clearances, Birlinn, 2013, p48

needed to earn decent livings off this land? Or was it simply progress and a little active encouragement of a migration that was good for everyone with happy ex peasants given the chance to prosper in new lands? The truth is, almost certainly, that it depended on who you were, where you were and the local circumstances. If you were young, lucky and high enough in status to have had your own lease then getting a bit of cash in exchange for leaving the land would sometimes have meant a chance for freedom, adventure and greater prosperity. If you were elderly or too poor to have been anything but a hired hand then being turned out of your community and your support network would have left you without everything in your life that you understood and valued and little chance of coping with the change.

The clearance of the upper part of the Dee mainly happened around the late 1820s but the experience for some must have been very similar to what was described by a geologist who witnessed the aftermath of a clearance elsewhere in 1854. As Geikie recalled it: "a strange wailing sound reached my ears at intervals on the breeze from the west …… I could see a long and motley procession winding along the road that led north ….. As I drew near I could see there were old men and women, too feeble to walk, who were placed in carts: the youngest members of the community on foot were carrying their bundles of clothes and household effects, while the children, with looks of alarm, walked alongside."[41]

The memory and the anger generated by events as visceral as this have lasted for generations and no amount of careful analysis of the 'inevitable' economic trends which drove them can remove the hurt. The upper reaches of the Dee are places where history matters. One whole way of life went and the one that replaced it was brought in from outside at significant cost. There can't be much doubt that the majority of current local residents would prefer to be making their living off the

---

[41] Ibid p2

back of tourists and wealthy temporary residents instead of from subsistence farming. Equally there can't be many people in Scotland who don't feel a strong sense that something morally questionable happened up here that ought not to be allowed to be forgotten or to be re-described with too much soft focus. Whole communities went and something very different replaced them.

The legacy for the modern visitor is considerably more positive. A landscape mostly given over to the rural sports of the very wealthy can provide the modern tourist with some interesting opportunities for exploration and some unexpected sights. I came into Braemar, the highest village on the Dee, over the Old Military Road on a glorious spring day. It had snowed heavily the day before and I had been in some doubt about whether I would make it over the pass. Instead the sun came out, the wind blew steadily from the south and I got treated to the sight of mountains decorated with fresh snow and an open and clear road. All along the route that the military had driven through this fearsomely difficult countryside there were six foot high polls topped with reflective strips. That was presumably so that drivers could still see where the road was meant to be when the snowdrifts got so deep that they obscured any signs of tarmac. I therefore expected the very summit of the road to be particularly bleak and abandoned. Not a bit of it. When I finally reached the top of the pass I found a busy ski resort with literally thousands of people taking full advantage of a generous April snow fall to get in some late skiing without having to burn any aviation fuel. People were busy enjoying themselves before getting the family back into their car and scurrying away back to the warmth of their hotel or their home.

It would not have been so much fun to be stuck up here in the snow if your job was to penetrate the Highlands and pacify resentful communities. There was little doubt about why the military wanted the road. Even with the advantage of General

Wade's fine construction it would still have been a hard march over dramatic countryside to get into this part of the Highlands. Back in 1715 when the Jacobite rebellion was getting underway "a better place for organising an uprising could not be imagined than Braemar"[42] It lay "in an inaccessible country, where there were no roads fit for horse, and far less for wheel carriages, artillery and provisions". So it proved relatively easy for the Jacobites to gather together in the inn where I stayed the night without worrying too much about disturbance from outsiders whilst they sent out calls for other Highlanders to come together and fight. Unfortunately for them it isn't possible to win a rebellion by sitting safely in remote countryside waiting for your enemy to gradually haul guns over the mountain passes. The rebels eventually had to brave the march down south. When they did so they ended up cut to pieces on the outskirts of Preston, executed in particularly imaginative and unpleasant ways in London, Lancashire or Scotland or, if they were really very lucky, creeping back home to keep their heads down in places like Braemar as they watched the military build the roads that were intended to make it a lot easier to beat them in future.

All of which leaves the history of the upper reaches of the Dee as something of a dilemma. It is a place with a long and proud track record of rebellion. Yet the old Highlanders in this part of Scotland were cleared off their land without the major riots that took place elsewhere in the country. It was at the very centre of a major uprising against English royalty. Yet it now hosts Balmoral Castle – one of the places where the current royal family is reputed to feel most at home. It has been prime hunting land for hundreds of years. Yet the vast majority of the hunting that takes place there now is very different to the deer hunts through wild forests that are recorded by early writers [43] The burnt moorland and beaten grouse shoots are

[42] Braemar, Stuart Erskine, (Edinburgh, 1898) p75
[43] Ibid p 10-12

part of a new tradition invented when the railways began to penetrate the Highlands and have little or nothing to do with ancient local practice and much more to do with social clubbing. Tradition has been invented to respond to external demand. The locals seem incredibly welcoming and work hard to give tourists a good time and to ensure they enjoy their visit to a remote and attractive location. But there is never much doubt that there is a clear distinction between locals and visitors and every now and then I thought I spotted healthy signs that those who belong here aren't entirely convinced that they ought to be obsequiously grateful for being patronised by the great and the good.

Braemar feels like a place that knows how to protect its own sense of identity under heavy pressure from tourism. It needs to be because it is so stunningly beautiful that it gets a lot of it. Early in the season, with crisp cold air, sunshine on snow-capped hills and a river running full of meltwater it was looking its very best and still comfortably quiet. I drove down to the Lin of Dee, left the car behind and set off walking to see how close I could get to the headwaters without putting the mountain rescue service to any trouble. I got there very early in the morning outside the main tourist season. So I had the path to myself. In two hours of walking up river I saw not a single person. Which was very much as I had planned. Some raw early spring air, the sight of a river wending its way across the bottom of a valley carved flat as a pancake by glaciers, and the mountains towering around me. What could have been finer? I even saw a group of ten stags taking advantage of the quiet to feed on the little patches of rough grass that clung on amidst the heather on the valley floor. There was no difficulty in determining that these were properly wild animals. In a country estate or a wildlife park the deer stare at you with a haughty lack of interest and go back to feeding as soon as they have taken a quick glance in your direction. These beasts checked me out every second of the time that I was within sight. The biggest stag positioned himself at the front of the group with his antlers proudly on display and even though I must have been 100 yards away his eyes never left me and he wanted me to know that if I made any move in his direction I would be trouble. I stuck to walking calmly along the path trying to look relaxed and unthreatening as I tried to work out why ten males were together. I came to the conclusion that it was time for the women to give birth and they wanted to be well away from troublesome argumentative males before they did the job in privacy. Consequently, the males were well down on testosterone and happy to group together for safety.

There wasn't much other wildlife out there in the cold at this time of year. The snow line began about two hundred feet above the path making it too cold for most insects. Few insects meant few birds and a lot of quiet. At first the path had gone through pine forest. Not natural pine forest – but plantations that mainly consisted of regimented trees all of the same age. An absence of decaying wood in the undergrowth and the natural protective oils within the pine left little for any wildlife to eat. It had therefore been something of a relief when I emerged from the plantations to get the full advantage of a magnificent vista opening up ahead of me. In front of me I could see miles of open countryside and a strong broad river winding its way across a valley floor. It curved gently from one side of that valley to the other across a bed of stones. On either side this stretch of the Dee was bordered by washed out peat bogs, bilberry and heather plants, and the occasional bit of very scrubby grass. A broad well-made path had been driven straight and clear across that wide area of heathland. Nothing obstructed the view of the river disappearing into the mountains in the distance and the path heading the same way. It looked wonderful with the snow covering much of the heights, and then different shades of green, brown and russet covering the lower slopes and the valley floor.

Before the trees were cut down, and the deer nibbled the tasty buds and new grown bark off any tender new shoots and prevented their return, those views would not have been so open. High up on some of the steepest land I could still see a few small pine plantations showing just how far into the hills the natural tree cover was supposed to spread. It's absence made for great long distance views but not for particularly rich ecology. In the opinion of those who have studied the natural ecology:

"Originally the slopes would have been covered by dense woodland, part of the great forest of Caledonia which stretched, with gaps for the highest mountains, from coast to coast. … On the best soils of the deeper river valleys, … oak would have been the commonest tree in a mixed deciduous forest, of oak, ash, hazel and wych elm with smaller amounts of bird cherry, aspen, glean, alder and willows. The wild wood contained more dead standing timber than is usual today, and some of the mature trees would have reached a considerable age."[44]

Nothing remotely like that remains. Lower down the river, where it is easier to make an impact, a lot of excellent work is being done by some very energetic agencies to restore and protect a more natural landscape. Here, in the mountains, the countryside is harder to restore and the main reason that the long-distance walkers and off-road cyclists can enjoy dramatic views of the landscape is because it has been stripped of its natural cover.

On this particular morning this meant that I got all the benefit of the simple pleasure of walking along a good clear path that let me raise my head and look far into the distance as I strode out. Eventually I reached a point where two large tributaries merged and I followed the Dee as it came in from the north. It began to be more of an upland stream and less of a gentle river babbling over shallows. The hills started to close in on the

[44] Peter Marren, A Natural History of Aberdeen, (Callender, Haughend, Finzean, Aberdeen, 1982) p 13

valley and both the path and the valley sides became progressively steeper. Before long I reached the snowline and it was quickly very clear that if I went any further then I was going to have to head into the highest parts of the Cairngorms. On my own, two days after a heavy snowfall, with the first signs of drizzle coming in from the West I decided that this was as far as I could safely go to get a feel for the source of the Dee.

On the walk back I saw one couple striding confidently past me into those hills but felt no guilt about abandoning any illusions about making my own attempt on the summit. I had set off before breakfast to get the best of the morning weather and was now more than ready to take full advantage of restoring whatever calories I had burned. Despite retracing my steps the long distance views were every bit as stunning. Having turned around I was now staring at a different set of mountains and the view of the river heading down towards the gaps between them was every bit as impressive as the sight of it coming out of all that barren moorland and snow. The deer had left their early morning feeding site and moved on to somewhere more secluded and as I approached the car park it became clear why. What had been a rather isolated place with one other car in it had begun to turn into a much busier location. Twenty or so cars had arrived. There were people walking their kids and trying to get them to share their enjoyment of the countryside. There were people riding bikes up some very rugged terrain. There were walkers carefully lacing boots that appeared to be the product of some very high tech design work and an equal emphasis on fashion. And there were folks just pootling about by the water throwing the occasional stone into the river. In short everyone seemed to be enjoying themselves and so was I. This is a very good place to go exploring and it was a genuine pleasure to see how many people were determined to do as much of that as they were comfortable with and then spend a bit of cash in the local shops and cafes. I went back to Braemar, found myself a very nice breakfast lunch at a café overlooking the Clunie Water as it tumbles its last few yards into the Dee and felt very pleased with myself for getting out early.

At the other end of the Dee things could scarcely be more different. Instead of open countryside and the company of large numbers of holidaymakers you find yourself enclosed in a busy city environment. The mouth of the Dee is the business end of the river. I set out to explore it by walking the last few miles of the river banks and started out from a well restored set of leisure gardens called Duthie Park. The moment I left the gardens it quickly became clear that around here the river is no longer preserved primarily for pleasure but is there to serve a useful purpose. A busy road with fast traffic ran right alongside the Dee and the few joggers that were brave enough to run along the river banks were taking in more than their fair share of petrol fumes. Despite all that benzine I could just about smell the flavour of the sea. There was seaweed growing from some of the rocks near the tide line but the tide was out and a broad strong river was running rapidly down towards the ocean. I didn't have to follow it for long before the riverside walk took me across a couple more busy roads and right up to the gates of the modern docks. Some very impressive ships were being loaded with complicated machinery and equipment ready to head out to the North Sea rigs. They seemed to dwarf the bright yellow speed boats that were slung around their decks so that they could nip rapidly in and around those rigs when they made it out to the oil and gas fields.

Around the corner I found the Maritime Museum where there was a scale model of one of these rigs. I quickly realised the scale of what has happened out in the depths of the North Sea. The rigs dwarf the ships that had impressed me every bit as comprehensively as the ships dwarfed the little speedboats. Oil platforms are the size of a small industrial estate. They aren't simple little structures supporting a drill and a few other bits and pieces. The scale model of the Tern Alpha Rig that the museum was using as a centrepiece stretched up four stories and dominated the whole museum. The original was 283 metres in height from the bottom of the North Sea to the top of the rig. I make that the equivalent of a 45 storey building rising out of the sea in an astonishing feat of engineering. Whatever you think of the merits of powering a civilisation by extracting fossils that have taken millions of years to form from under the ocean and then burning them in seconds to warm up the planet there is no doubting the skills of the engineers that pull off the job of getting at that oil and gas. Out there in the wilds of one of the toughest seas they've managed to create steel structures on a gigantic scale that have been able to withstand decades of battering by the wind and the waves.

The work required to service the oil and gas industry now dominates the port of Aberdeen. It wasn't always so. Go back far enough and the estuary of the Dee wasn't much use as a harbour. A river that runs down from high mountains carrying a lot of silt doesn't scour out good deep water or even leave its sandbanks in the same place for very long. One bad winter and the sands at the mouth of the Dee had a dangerous tendency to move about in ways that no river pilots could reliably predict. So Aberdeen wasn't always viewed as the best port on this coastline. It took a whole series of gradual improvements culminating in a re-routing of the whole river in the 1870s to get the Dee sufficiently under control and to force it to run out to the sea between two great breakwaters.[45] That work enabled 400 Herring Boats to head out to sea in a single year from this harbour. It also made it possible for large numbers of whaling boats to set sails for Greenland and for steam powered trawlers to bring in large quantities of cod and haddock.

---

[45] Scotland's East Coast Fishing Industry, Mark I'Anson, (Stenlake Publishing, Ayrshire, 2008) p26

There is no difficulty finding the traces of this history in the streets around the docks. I walked past the Seamen's Mission, a Norwegian sailor's church, the Shore Porter's Wharehouses, and roads with names that easily communicated what their particular specialism had been. Weigh Street and Baltic Square don't require much interpretation or imagination and I was soon able to conjure up a vision of bustling trade. But it was after I'd walked past most of the historical buildings bordering the docks and was in a much more uninspiring collection of modern industrial units that I got a more direct understanding of life at the mouth of the river in the days just after the new docks had been created. Stuck in the middle of endless streets of companies supplying specialist equipment for the oil and gas industry I found St Clements Church situated rather forlornly between an industrial estate, a dockyard and a warehouse. It was closed and boarded up and looked like it had not been in use for many years. It's graveyard was in slightly better condition and proved to be really interesting. The people who had buried their relatives here had made good use of the headstones to communicate some of the realities of the lives they lived.

Ann Croughton died in 1865 at the age of 59. Which sounds pretty good. Especially as one of her sons, a shipmaster made it to 69 and died in 1909. Yet her son William was lost at sea in 1869 aged 28. Her daughter Charlotte died aged 22 the same year. Son Daniel lived until he was 27. The gravestone tells us that he went to the bottom along with all on board the Strathway on 1st Feb 1900. This was not unusual. Thomas Walls was a fish curer and perhaps felt a little safer as he was working on shore. Yet his father "drowned at sea by the upturning of his boat" in 1899. Thomas seems to have had three children who all died in infancy and were buried with him. There is no mention on the stone of any children living into adulthood. The gravestones don't just reveal personal tragedies they also provide insights into what people were doing for a living. I noticed the grave of a shipbuilder and of a man who had worked his whole life for the Great North Railroads. The local blacksmith died at the age of 35 and the local painter, Alexander Kath, was even more fortunate as he had made it to 72 when he eventually died in 1852. Four years later a merchant with the glorious name of Absolom Poulter died at the age of 70. Presumably in his bed. Andrew Baxter was less fortunate. He died a very long way from home in the cold waters of Port Elizabeth aged 26 in 1894. The location indicates that he was trying to catch a whale.

The neglected graveyard at St Clements Church had clearly once been THE place to be buried if you were a person of some standing in trade in this city. Now it gave a sharp lesson in how very much times have changed. This city has seen a whole series of booms and busts in the bounty of the seas. For many years herring was landed in numbers that seemed inexhaustible. They supported not just the livelihoods of the fishermen but a small army of women who earned their living gutting and salting the fish. The remains of the guts were used to make fertiliser and the fish itself was enjoyed [46]as a staple food source by millions either in the form of very tasty pickles or as breakfast kippers.[47] Then technology improved and they became easier to find and to catch and within a couple of decades they were fished out so badly that they have still not returned in anything remotely like their former abundance.[48] There was a period when the whaling industry supplied good enough money to seem well worth the risk of sailing into dangerous waters and trying to skewer a monster from a little rowing boat. That resource also ran out. The men who sailed on the Lady Franklin out of Aberdeen in 1853 returned in 1854 with 27 bowhead whales and made 174 tons of oil out of their labours. That must have seemed worth the risk of ending up in that graveyard or under a very cold sea. In 1870 I doubt

---

[46] Ocean of Life, Callum Roberts, (Allen Lane, London) p315
[47] For a fun account of the Herring industry and its associated traditions see Herring Tales, Donald Murray, (Bloomsberry, 2015)
[48] Callum Roberts, op cit p49

whether those who sailed in the Kate felt quite so pleased with life when they trailed back into port after a hard winter without having caught a single whale.[49] It had taken less than a couple of decades to decimate the natural resource. Or rather worse than that. To decimate means to kill every tenth one. This was more like the other way round. Less than one out of every ten bowheads was still alive in the fishing grounds. A bowhead can live for 200 years and reproduces very slowly.

Now the city is watching and waiting for the signs that its latest trade might also be coming to a close. The first drilling for oil and gas around here began in 1966 and when I was at school in the late 60s I remember being taught how wealthy the United Kingdom was going to become if they discovered serious reserves of oil and gas. Back then the UK was producing only 86,000 tonnes of crude oil from a couple of tiny onshore sites. By the end of the twentieth century we were producing 137,099,000 tonnes and exporting 46,928,000 more than we imported[50]. That is an astonishing transformation in such a short period of time. It fuelled significant employment in and around the mouth of the Dee. Some of those jobs are in warm comfortable places doing the legal work, the accountancy generated by the industry or simply providing restaurants and homes for the workers. Many of the jobs are not so safe and secure. They can be every bit as dangerous as the old traditional fishing and whaling jobs out in the harsh seas. One hundred and sixty-nine people lost their lives in the Piper Alpha disaster 120 cold miles north east of Aberdeen when an explosion on a rig created a gas and oil fireball. It takes time to get rescue crews out to places that remote and there aren't many safe places on a burning oil rig that far out in the ocean. When they eventually got there two of the rescue crew lost their own lives bringing to safety the 61 workers who managed to survive. This was not the only

---

[49] Scottish Arctic Whaling, Chesley Sanger, (Birlinn, Edinburgh) p129
[50] Office of National statistics data

incident. There have been deaths in helicopter crashes, men lost at sea and a series of otherwise avoidable deaths of sick people who simply couldn't be got to treatment on shore quickly enough. It simply isn't possible to work in such a forbidding location and eliminate every risk.

The city of Aberdeen has a long tradition of risking life in order to earn a living. They also have a long history of seeing resources come and go. It is possible that the herring may one day return. It is possible that a new whaling industry can be built around tourist sightseeing trips. It is not possible that the oil or the gas can ever be restored once it has been used up and there is clear scientific evidence it is not wise to burn every last drop of it. So the hope around here must be that another more sustainable way of earning a living from high tech activities out at sea comes along in time to keep the city vibrant and prosperous. Efforts to construct massive wind turbines and get them securely positioned in the North Sea were underway whilst I was there. It is possible that the next high tech dangerous employment opportunity hereabouts will be offshore wind farming and that this might prove rather more sustainable than the previous ones.

Given the dependence on oil it wasn't entirely surprising that almost the last thing I saw as I approached the very mouth of the Dee was a large oil storage tank. It looked every bit as ugly as the huge gasometers that used to be prevalent all over the more neglected parts of our cities when gas was made out of coal and had to be stored locally. It was so near to the sea and I had walked past so much industrial activity that I assumed that this was how the river was going to end. I thought it might pour out into the sea besides a mess of industrial units in much the same way that the other Dee does. I could not have been more wrong. As I turned the corner across the street from the gas holder I suddenly found myself out of all the industrial landscape and in the middle of an utterly charming collection of houses nestling right on the sea front at the very end of the Dee.

This little community of stone dwellings huddled together to shut out the worst of the wind coming off the North Sea is known affectionately locally as Fittie. It didn't take me long to figure out that it hadn't got here as a result of organic growth of a fishing community but had been the product of some serious thought and planning. A normal fishing village is a chaos of different sizes, shapes and ages and rarely follows a grid pattern. This hamlet had been laid out by someone with an eye for regular ordered squares and straight lined streets and that person had used the back walls of the houses to enclose the whole development behind a protective barrier. Yet as soon as I walked through the outer protective walls into one of the charming little squares it quickly became evident that the occupants had every bit as strong a sense of individuality and rebellion as the planner had for order. Almost every house was decorated in its own eccentric style and accompanied by a 'tarry shed'. There was a glorious mix of regularly organised granite dwellings lining long straight paved walkways accompanied by a totally disorganised rabble of shed like out buildings plonked just across the pavement from the front doors. Each of the sheds is built from something different, has its own unique shape, has been painted in its own individual colour and seems to be used to suit quaint quirks of taste. A brightly decorated artist's studio sits next to a garden storage lean to with the paint peeling off and the wood cracking. A coal shed is positioned alongside a set of barbeque equipment. The contrast between these chaotic temporary structures and the stark solid granite of the buildings made for some fantastic visual discontinuities. It was like someone had tried to shoe horn a set of interestingly argumentative people into a ponderously well-ordered plan and those awkward people had rebelled and made sure that they expressed themselves with determination and insisted on creating some fun and some individuality in their lives.

When I read up on the community it seemed that this was indeed pretty much what had happened. There had been some fishing homes around this area for centuries, taking advantage of being right next to the harbour and on the sea front. Then in 1809 the Superintendent of Public Works, John Smith, had done his best to make sure that good quality sturdy homes were provided for fishing families and had done so with a well-conceived planned development of 28 homes. It was good worthy work and provided much better accommodation for hard working locals than they had ever seen before. His concept of trying to provide one home for each family and then protecting the community inside safe small squares where everyone could spill out onto the street and mix happily seems to have been a success. It was added to and expanded by later planners and they further improved the standard of the homes but the essential design remained firmly in place because it worked. Then the families started adding their own little touches by dragging drift wood off the beach or acquiring other cheap materials before using them to give themselves a little extra added space in whatever fashion they felt like. Anarchy mixed nicely with order and resulted in a set of homes that is a joy to walk around and explore.

These days there aren't many traditional fishing families left in ownership and the houses have become very desirable for anyone who likes to live somewhere a bit different and enjoys mixing closely with their neighbours. The pictures of the place in the 19th century are very different. They show groups of women sitting outside these homes wearing rough clothing busy gutting herring. It is tempting to look at those images and imagine lives of bleak harshness for these women. That isn't entirely misplaced as there can be no doubt that fish gutting was back breaking hard work that carried high risk of injury from sharp knives cutting desperately cold fingers by mistake. Yet there was also a very different side to the fish wives' existence. You could earn good money for the times if you were capable of gutting herring with speed and skill. You didn't do it wearing your Sunday best and most of the week you looked one hell of a sight as you splattered yourself with fish innards. But you earned your own money and the right to a bit of independence. People looked down on fishwives as rough elements who would readily give you the harsh edge of their tongue. The fishwives may well have seen it rather differently. They had a proud defiance that stemmed from the knowledge that they were doing a job that brought the money in. If you were the wife of a crofter at the top end of the Dee at the time of the Highland Clearances you didn't have a lot of control over what happened to you or a whole lot of choices about how your life panned out. If you were a fishwife from the foot of the Dee you had a certain amount of choice and freedom because the money you earned from desperately hard work gave you the right to a very loud and sassy say in what happened to you. Many herring gutters travelled up and down the East coast following the different shoals as they came close to shore and they picked up ideas and a lot of attitude along the way. They may have spent all week doing desperately hard work, dressed in the cheapest of clothing, experiencing horrible stenches and often living away from home in very rough accommodation but they could return to their neat homes in what is politely called Footdee with some money in their pocket and some pride. You didn't mess with a fishwife. She could fight her own corner.

Some of that defiance seems to have remained in the legacy. I wasn't the only tourist trying to explore the back streets of Fittee but it felt very clear that we were there on sufferance. No one seemed to mind you walking around and quietly glancing at their homes. Provided that you showed due respect. I got the distinct impression that if you gawped a bit too long and treated the residents like objects of curiosity you would get gawped at straight back and a pretty quick reminder of the ability of inheritors of the legacy of fishwife's pride to give every bit as good as they got. I liked that a lot. It felt like the river was trying to end very much as it began. Charm, beauty and character. A little eccentricity and some people who knew how to enjoy life.

I found a small gap in the protective grouping of the granite homes and walked through and discovered I had made it right onto the seafront. It was a busy place. People were walking their dogs, their kids or just themselves along an esplanade that stretched the whole sweep of a fine bay. A few brave souls were down on the sandy beach and some even braver ones were trying to learn to surf the succession of breakers that rolled in from the East. Right at the very end of the bay, where a protective wall kept the worst of the weather from the ships safely inside the harbour, an enterprising person had made a posh restaurant out of a former look-out tower that marked the very end of the Dee. I checked the prices and decided that it was aimed at people who were earning good money from the oil business. A few hundred yards up the coast an equally enterprising soul had parked a tea bar next to a welcoming bench. It was rather more within my budget so I sat for a long time cradling a cuppa and watched the ships and the people come and go. The Scottish Dee seemed to me to be ending in a much more enjoyable way than the Welsh one does.

The Welsh have a word for the mouth of a river. It is Aber. So, for example, Swansea is on the river Tawe and is known in Welsh as Abertawe. Aberystwyth is on the river Ystwyth and Aberavon is near the river Afan. Logically the Welsh name for a city built at the mouth of the river Dee would be Aberdeen. Somehow the Scottish city had ended up with the Welsh name. Those Celts got around a bit and it would be nice to think that they left their mark in a name just as clearly as the fish wives had in a legacy of community.

Downham

There are two Downham estates. One of them is a huge housing development built by the old London County Council to provide quality housing for those who might otherwise not have been able to afford it. The other is a country estate in Lancashire where the aristocratic owners control the lease on every significant property in the village and its surroundings. One encapsulates urban development and an attempt to build a better future for Londoners living in crowded dwellings. The other is the epitome of rural quiet. No television aerials were ever allowed to spoil the roof lines of the homes in Downham Lancashire. The owner of every home didn't like looking at them. So for a long time the locals had to make do with poor reception or listening to their radios whilst the rest of the viewing nation tucked in to their TV dinners and got familiar with the characters in Coronation Street. A small price to pay for ensuring the people in the big house could look out over the moors without being reminded that the world was changing. Eventually the owners relented and installed underground cables at considerable expense.

Ironically if you ban all evidence that TV exists from a village it turns it into an ideal location for TV cameras. No one wants to be filming their latest historical drama only to discover that the viewers can see TV aerials poking out from the roof lines of what are meant to be 18th century homes. Better by far to set your cameras up in a village that has kept development at arms' length. Downham has done that in spades.

I began my tour there on a cold Monday morning in February which had the considerable advantage that the normal hordes of tourists were absent and the serious disadvantage that a nagging wind coming in from the West was all too clearly present. I stood on the steps of the church and wrapped my coat tightly around me. The view was a considerable compensation. It is dominated by one great dramatic feature. Pendle Hill looms above the village. Calling it a hill doesn't do it justice. It is a great slab of hard rock covered by thin acid moorland and it is a serious enterprise to walk to the top. On a dry day in summer, a popular local activity is to arrive in a car at the easiest place to climb it. Most people then proceed to exchange pleasantries with their fellow climbers as they work their way up a well-marked path. Usually you can see some desperately unfit people in high heels trying to tackle an unfamiliar challenge. Often you are left in no doubt that some of the children being dragged up there are doing so under serious protest whilst others are enjoying every minute and having a fine time of it. The Downham side of the hill is, however, a place that few people choose to climb. It is steeper and the path is much less well trodden. If the mist comes down and you are stuck up there without a compass, a good map and a lot of experience you are in trouble. So this part of the moorland is mainly left to the local farmers who have to get up and out onto it in all weathers. It takes a lot of skill and not a little determination to make a living out of rearing sheep on this chunk of rock.

Nevertheless, the same high ground that made for hard upland farming also gave the locals some much easier territory to look after and turn to productive use. The village nestles beneath the mountain, gaining protection from the worst of the wind. Reliable streams of clean hill water rattle down from Downham Moor and begin to turn more gentle as the ground starts to flatten out and they run past the houses. They have carried down enough soil over the eons to mean that this has been prosperous farming land for a very long time. You could raise your animals on the wild moors, grow your oats and vegetables on good silt soil in the valley and get whatever produce was surplus to requirements out to market easily enough by following excellent long distance trading routes. As a consequence of that fortunate combination, the houses have a sense of solidity and affluence about them. They are built out of the hard local stone which was cut into great rectangular chunks to make walls and simply sliced more thinly if the builders wanted a roofing tile. This gives a consistency of colour and texture to the buildings. They are all as grey and dark as the skyline was today. Curiously this stark colour doesn't in any way ruin the look of the homes. Instead it gives them a feeling of belonging here. They seem to have come out of the ground by a natural process and to gather together into interesting little groups. Rooflines intersect at strange angles and large wealthy homes have become mixed in with short terraces of workers cottages in ways that seemed to represent a healthily varied community. There may, in times gone by, have been one very rich owner, some solidly well-off farmers and several dirt poor workers but at least they met each other and knew something of each other's lives. These days the single ownership has the advantage that second home ownership can be controlled so that, despite turning into a significant tourist attraction, the village still retains a real sense of community.

As I stood in the church yard looking down on the houses rain began to sweep across the valley in pulses. I retreated inside. I soon came across evidence that the village had been working hard on its community spirit for a long time. The church had some interesting local history documents, one of which described the Downham Benevolent Society. It turned out that the working men of the village formed a friendly society back in 1785, paying a shilling each to give themselves some insurance against hard times and tuppence each to have some fun. It was, of course, intended to be good clean fun, controlled and managed by a committee of the respectable and respected. Fighting, drunkenness and bringing disorder were not allowed and members were expected to lead a sober life. You also weren't allowed in if you had venereal disease but how exactly they proposed to check this was not made entirely clear by the rule book drawn up in 1795. What it did spell out is that there were to be no stone getters, miners, soldiers or seamen admitted to the society. Clearly the Benevolent Society wasn't benevolent towards everyone.

There is a long history of snobbery and a determination to ensure that the better kind of labourer isn't confused with their less prosperous neighbours. Or forced to mix with their womenfolk when serious business was afoot. Women weren't allowed in.

The church itself provided plenty of reminders of the status of different people within the community. One name dominated. There are plaques recording the memory of several members of Assheton family. The family vault is under the floor of the south east corner of the church. It sits underneath the Assheton chapel. There is a window in memory of an Assheton, who also gets honoured in the pulpit itself. Oh, and of course the very church itself is a memory to them as they had most of it knocked down and rebuilt in 1910. As an exercise in reminding people, at least once a week, that one family owned all the land hereabouts it must have been very effective. Most Lancashire villages have a plethora of different churches created by ordinary working people who were fiercely loyal to their own distinct sect whose members were particularly proud of dissenting from the official religion and striking up their own independent relationship with their own idea of God. Here I could only find evidence of one church. So you got your religion in whatever form the big family felt best.

Religion has been going strong here for a very long time. Though the church is mostly new – after all a hundred years counts as modern when it comes to religious buildings – there has been one on this site for great chunks of time. There is reputed to have been a Saxon church here and the consensus is that over a thousand years is a reliable date for when worship here began. When the rain eased off and I was able to explore further afield it was quickly easy to see why. The church stands yards from a Roman road. Which itself exploited a long-distance route which had been in use much earlier.

Walking a few hundred yards outside the village to the north and the east I came across the remains of this Roman road running proudly across the top of a rise heading straight across the Pennines. They had chosen dry ground and built drainage channels either side of it and I stood for a while in the middle of their construction and watched it stretch out towards the east. It clearly represents a very substantial piece of work that ran for many miles. I was looking across a wide gentle valley that had been cut by the strong flow of the river Ribble. The gradients here didn't need to be particularly steep or difficult in order to force a straight road through from one town to the next. The map shows the Roman route sometimes hidden beneath more recent country lanes and sometimes still exposed on open countryside but always heading firmly from one important location to the next as it travels right across the Pennines. This is the narrowest part of the north of England and the passes through the mountains aren't as steep as elsewhere. It has therefore always been the logical way to travel by land from the coast facing Ireland to the coast facing Norway. Head further north and the journey across Britain is a lot longer because of the great bulge of the Lake District. Head further south and the land widens again and is quite a bit steeper. Here you could get across the country following the clear easy landmarks like Pendle Hill and make a nice profit on moving goods from one place to the next.

I followed a footpath down off the Roman's version of this route and walked between dramatic outcrops of rock towards the village mill. I can't say that I was entirely surprised to discover that this building had been owned by the Assheton family. If you were going to control a town and make good money then it is a pretty good idea to own the mill as well as the church. This one was no longer working but had instead been turned into a domestic home with the mill race clearly evident behind it. I followed the footpath past the house and alongside a long straight stretch of water which in the past had drawn most of the flow off from a nearby stream in order to ensure that there was a reliable source of water tumbling onto the waterwheel and driving the huge millstones. After the mill closed the thin mill pond had fallen into disuse and become just a boggy mess but a lot of work had been done relatively recently to restore it properly and there was now no mistaking the canal like structure. Sensibly the conservers had avoided the mistake of making it too well manicured and chosen instead to let local wildlife colonise it. As a result it looked like it had always remained intact and it sat completely naturally in the countryside. The reeds, the weeds and the watercourse formed a perfect backdrop for the old mill.

I walked past them up the stream. The ground underfoot had been made damp by the rain and churned up by the feet of cattle but it was worth the work of picking my way through the wet patches. The path followed the stream through a delightful little valley with mature trees and constantly changing views. Wherever it came up to the edge of the brook it became possible to see little swirl pools of deep clear water, interspersed with wider sections where the flow worked its way between large rocks. It was easy to visualise these rocks being swept down the hillside and left here by one of the regular torrents that pour down whenever storms hit Pendle Hill. Most had been in the water long enough to have become rounded and softened but a few still showed the sharper edges of more recent arrival. The path was clear and some charming wooden bridges had been built to ease the way across any tributaries that threatened to block off the route. Not a single person passed me as I walked and the only sound seemed to be the aggressive squawking of crows arguing in the tree tops. Whenever the path climbed a little my eyes were quickly drawn towards the dominating presence of Pendle Hill. Then the route would head back into the depths of the valley again and not even that monster could be seen above the steep sides. I felt enclosed in the countryside and privileged to be able to stand still on occasion and simply absorb the cleansing effect of the gentle sounds of the water and the wind. Way in the distance some agricultural machinery was working but there were no planes in the sky, and it felt like I had got a very fair share of my own private time and space in a countryside which is actually very busy.

It was therefore with a degree of regret that I followed the path away from the steam and back towards the village. I was now walking across open fields alongside a place where the hedgerows had been removed to make it easier to farm the land. This is a controversial practice as it means the loss of a lot of important habitat for wildlife in order to make it a little easier for agricultural machinery to get to every corner of the land. In times past the controversy ran in a different direction. A lot of the locals were very upset indeed when hedgerows and other barriers were erected way back in the 16th century in order to keep them out of land that they had been using for a very long time. Enclosure here wasn't an amicable process. Downham Green had been one great common ground and Richard Assheton was accused of having a "malicious and covetous mind" when he decided to close 40 acres of it off with a great ditch and hedge in the 16th century. Before many years had passed people from nearby Chatham had become so annoyed at losing opportunities on this land that they "assembled in warlike array, together with a great number of the women of Chatburn, and broke down his wall of enclosure, so that he had no profit from it." Their resistance didn't work. By 1590 only about 30 acres of the green were left open.[51]

The modern village is very popular with tourists as the long ownership of everything by one important local family has left us with an interesting heritage. But hidden beneath the chocolate box appearance of what is a genuinely very pleasant location there is a rather starker history. The heritage came at a price for those who were pushed off the land. They lost the right to do simple things like cut limestone and burn it to create quicklime. They lost access to firewood or to grazing and hunting rights. The land became a lot more productive for

---

[51] http://www.british-history.ac.uk/vch/lancs/vol6/pp552-558

the new owners and helped fund a lifestyle that could maintain the grand manor house that sits alongside the generously rebuilt church. But the land was now firmly under the control of one family. It is charming for the modern visitor to see homes that have never been allowed to be cluttered up by television aerials and where change has been carefully managed. Yet management also involved control. It might be cosy and comfortable to believe that England had once consisted of a network of small villages like Downham where the Lord of the Manor knew everyone and looked after their best interests. The truth is a lot messier and provides less grounds for nostalgia. The land that this village sits on was enclosed against stiff resistance. Time has not always stood still here. Something very dramatic took place in the 16th century and the descendants of those who fought hard against that change have had to live in the shadow of it for a very long time. The Downham Estate in Lancashire looks nice – but even in the cosiest communities where the landowners have sought to offer the most benevolent support for the local community you don't have to look far beneath the surface to find a very long history of power and powerlessness.

****

The Downham Estate on the borders of Lewisham and Bromley was inspired by people who believed they were making a real start on putting an end to all of that. The least that those who built this huge council estate thought that they might achieve was to make sure that the some of the more respectable elements of the poor and the underprivileged of London were well housed. It was constructed between the wars to enable 30,000 Londoners to escape the inner-city slums and to let them get out to the suburbs where they could live better and richer lives. Instead of being crammed into narrow streets and small tenements the working class would have proper indoor plumbing, dry healthy bedrooms, a garden where vitamin filled fruit and vegetables could be grown and spaces where children could play.

The idea that workers deserved to be provided with decent housing and that doing so would improve their lives and their characters goes right back to Owen's model village and beyond. It grew in strength throughout the nineteenth century, not just through the example of the many other experimental communities built by benevolent factory owners, but also via mutual support groups such as building societies. It gained support on the right of the political spectrum from enthusiasts for healthy citizens of the empire such as Joseph Chamberlin. He rose to prominence and popularity by the simple expedient of helping to provide the good people of Birmingham with useful services like gas, water and sewage disposal so that they could rest easier in their homes. It was an important strand of belief for the Arts and Crafts movement which contained many people who were inspired by the idea that ordinary working people deserved to have some beauty and comfort in their domestic lives as well as in their labour. And it was a powerful part of the convictions held by almost all the turn of the century socialists. When the First World War produced a couple of revolutions in Russia, waves of mutinies in the French army, then industrial unrest, rent strikes and even police strikes in Britain, mainstream policy makers on almost all sides of the political spectrum began to realise that they might be wise to create 'homes for heroes'. The idea of constructing council housing and of providing decent garden suburb estates grew steadily in popularity and was expressed in waves of legislation that first permitted a few brave and well financed councils to build homes and rent them out and then encouraged and financed the vast majority to do so.

The extent of the dedication showed by some of those involved in trying to improve housing for working people in big cities is hard to exaggerate. Take, for example, the work of the

Salter's in Bermondsey. Instead of living in comfort and then working occasionally in poor communities they chose to live right in the middle of one of those communities. The husband worked as a doctor and gained such a reputation for honestly helping local people that they voted him in as their MP. The wife, Ada Salter, also focused on good practical helpful measures – the main one of which was housing. As a result of her efforts, and the couple's determination to both work and live in the community they wished to help, enormous strides were made in the quality of housing available to the people of Bermondsey. It was work which cost her and her husband dearly. Their only child died at the age of 8 of scarlet fever[52]. This wasn't the first time the child had caught it. Twice before she had caught a disease that was prevalent in poor areas of Bermondsey but not in the wealthier parts of London where her parents could easily have afforded to live. With admirable commitment the couple stayed put and persisted with their chosen task even after their own hearts had been ripped out. Not surprisingly, that kind of self-sacrifice over decades from a couple of honest politicians was widely admired in the locality. Ada became Mayor of the local council.

The planners from the London County Council who set out to design and build the model community of the Downham estate almost certainly also thought that they were also doing something worthwhile with their working lives. Even if not too many of them were prepared to live in their creation themselves. It took over a decade of dedicated work by determined officials to get the estate built. The idea for constructing it came about shortly after the war but it was only in 1920 that suitable land was purchased. It then took ten more years for the first 6,000 houses to get completed and it was not until 1937 that the next 1,038 were put up. Going from a concept to getting the money and the permissions

---

[52] See the excellent Ada Salter, Pioneer of Ethical Socialism, Graham Taylor (Lawrence & Wishart, London, 2016) p102

needed in order to get it built has never been easy. In the years between coming up with the idea for the scheme and actually building it those planners had to cope with frequent changes in the rules and the funding as the country went through a succession of Prime Minsters and Liberal, Labour and Conservative politicians – each of whom came up with different ideas and put them into law.[53] But eventually persistence from the London County Council planners paid off. A huge area near to Bromley went from being farmland and a rifle range to being covered by homes for 30,000 people.

Going from an idea to a practical reality also involves a lot of compromises. The vision of the developers was a garden suburb of high quality homes delightfully laid on in gracious curves around a central park and recreation area with schools for the children close at hand. Design was inspired by the Arts and Crafts movement. From the air or on a map it is easy to see their intentions. Straight lines and rows of boring terraces have been avoided. A long central street, called Downham Way, snakes past a bewildering variety of differently shaped side streets. There are cul de sacs, there are loops, there are arcs and every now and then there are a few straight lines thrown in for good measure. The whole creation clusters around the two large open spaces of Downham Fields and Downham Playing Fields with the clear intention of providing the residents with access to a little taste of country living. They called it a Cottage Estate.

However, good quality housing doesn't come cheap - even if it is built on the edge of the city on land that doesn't cost a lot. The ideal features that the designers wanted started to look a bit expensive and there were worries about the impact on rents for residents as well as over council finances. There was a lot of scrimping and saving on the original vision. I was

---

[53] See Council Housing and Culture, Alison Ravetz, (Routledge, 2008) pages 85-95 for an account of the steady stream of changing legislation and its impact

therefore very curious to see how many of the ideals had survived the budget cuts and stood up to the test of time.

The first thing that struck me as I got off the train at Grove Park station and walked onto the estate was a feeling of familiarity. Up and down the country a large number of council estates were built on similar principles. The main streets are wide, the gardens are generous, and the homes are clustered together into a series of short terraces designed to give occupants some sense of belonging to a particular location instead of being dumped into one huge anonymous whole. You are left in no doubt that you are on a single estate created for a purpose. All the roof heights tend to be the same on any one street and the materials are also pretty consistent. Here, on the Downham Estate, the occasional pebble dash finish has crept in but the vast majority of the homes are brick fronted with rectangular windows. Give a few well practiced bricklayers a job like this to do and it won't take them long to bash out a lot of brickwork at a very reasonable rate. Two teams of brickies were able to put up one of these houses in only two weeks and do it to a decent standard[54]. Most of the rest of the construction process was made equally straightforward. No self-respecting carpenter would be held up for long making doors and windows to these designs and several of the features were chosen because they were easy to mass produce in a factory and then slot into place on site. Indeed, some of the homes were entirely prefabricated and merely assembled like a kit[55]. The roofing designs are every bit as efficient. The tilers could progress at real speed between one house and the next across nice easy straight lines.

Most of the work of those highly skilled labourers looked to me to be standing up to the test of time well. Eighty years of British winters haven't done too much damage and the

---

[54] Antonia Rubenstein, Just Like the Country, Age Exchange 1991, p19
[55] Ibid, p20

majority of the houses look to be in a perfectly reasonable state of repair. The same can't always be said for the plots of land that surround them. Out the front of many of the houses there are short, often rather messy gardens, where bins have been left out for collection. Several of the buildings had 'To Let' signs outside them. Elsewhere gardens have been ripped up to provide a bit of hardstanding to park a car on. To the rear the plan to get the working masses busy growing their own food seems to have proved a mixed blessing. I got an occasional glimpse of a large plot of messy weeds which the occupant had more or less given up trying to maintain. Yet it was also possible to find signs that someone had found joy in working for many hours on transforming their plot into a little bit of paradise.

That tension between the existence of green spaces and the cost in time and effort to maintain them properly becomes even more evident as soon as you leave the Downham Way and walk through the quieter side streets. I kept coming across unexpected open areas. One street would have a children's playground. Another a large rectangular lawn surrounded by lines of mature trees separating one side of a residential street from another. Trees that had grown enormously since the 1930s and were now substantial presences dwarfed some of the houses, starving them of light. Each crossroad or junction seemed to have its own shape of open grassland spreading out around it. The distances between homes were astonishingly generous compared to what any developer of even the most expensive of estates would provide for today's new residents.

There was grass and there were trees everywhere. Yet in many places all this greenery didn't feel like it was enhancing the appearance of the estate. An awful lot of it felt like it was in a bad state of repair and was suffering from poor maintenance. There were frequent notices telling me that fly tippers would be prosecuted. The fact that these ugly notices were necessary didn't inspire confidence. The planners had wanted residents to walk through a garden suburb taking pleasure in being uplifted by the feel of the country penetrating into the city. I was in danger of being cast down by a feel of neglect. Not consistent unmitigated neglect. More a peculiar mixture of quiet suburban pride of place from some residents and can't be bothered from others. Half repaired cars sat rusting in some drives whilst others had displays of pot plants that would do any garden centre proud. Some of the communal spaces were being looked after and protected for the community – others were simply looking tatty because it was beyond the capacity of either the council or the local community to keep so much in good order. Somehow the bold determination of the planners to create a green community has resulted in a strange feeling that the place was rather empty. Instead of adding grace and charm to the development the wide streets and large areas of grassland seemed to suck the energy out of the streets.

That lack of energy contrasted sharply with the views some parts of the estate provided across the whole of the busy centre of the city of London. This part of the suburbs is surprisingly high and it provides astonishing views down onto some of the tallest buildings in Britain. I found myself standing on a near deserted street looking down on a complex mix of super modern skyscrapers where people were rushing about and money was being made. It was hard to recognise the two places as part of the same working city. Most of the people who were earning their living had headed off to battle with the crowds down below leaving the streets up here to the a few elderly people and the occasional mother with a push chair.

I began to become disorientated by wondering between the different deserted backstreets. The houses varied in size and in shape but all seemed to have come from the same pattern book so that I was never quite sure whether I was in somewhere new or going back down the street where I had just been. I felt confused and swallowed up by the estate with shocking completeness. It wasn't an entirely comfortable experience. I felt I was drowning in an amorphous mass of featureless similarity that led nowhere and was hard to escape from. Then suddenly I turned a corner and found a path out onto Downham Fields and with a sense of relief I emerged from the labyrinth.

Like many parks these fields aren't just here because the planners wanted to provide as much open space as they could. The two prime open spaces on the estate were very difficult places to build. A stream ran through one of them and an awkwardly shaped hill dominated the other. So it was easier to leave them alone than it was to build on them. Nevertheless, it is pretty clear that these two parklands also represent a hugely significant statement of ambition from the planners. They didn't just want the new local residents to live in comfort in tree lined avenues, they wanted them to be able to walk through acres of open countryside at the weekend and get the full benefit of country living. They made very sure that the estate only had one pub but they also made sure that it had two very substantial parks. To this day the local school and the health and leisure centre back onto the park, providing users with a view over a decent amount of greenery despite living in what is now firmly part of the city.

The Leisure Centre is a rather fine modern building housing a very nice café that looks out over the park. As I sat and enjoyed my tea and cake three teenagers from the local West Indian community were using the next table to do their homework together. They seemed to be enjoying working through it and competing to show off how bright they were. A very elderly woman arrived at the counter and the woman serving her greeted her by name and then carefully carried over her purchases and made sure she was comfortably sat down. This was clearly a centre that was being well used by the community. So were the fields outside. People were out walking their dogs or jogging. The simple design concept of giving people a bit of relief from endless streets of housing and a chance to get out into the open air had worked well. It wasn't the finest park I've ever walked across but it was much more effective at doing the job it was intended to do than the little patches of rather tatty and grassland that dotted much of the rest of the estate. A huge mass of affordable housing had been broken up and provided with a focus.

For the first occupants, some of whom had been on the council house waiting list for almost a decade, the reaction to all this greenery was a lot more positive than mine. Most took to it like ducks to water and loved it from the first. Ron Chattlington's reaction is typical:

"We moved into a house opposite a farm .. you could just step over a ditch and be in the cabbages. Compared to the closeness of the East End, it was country - the spaciousness of Downham, it was absolutely beautiful."[56]

Others found the transition too much of a shock. Resident John Edwin Smith told a researcher that:

"There were quite a few families that came on the estate and never settled and they agitated to go. They went back to their old haunts."[57]

Most of the children seem to have found it a real pleasure to be able to head off and explore and their new school buildings were also a revelation. Phyllis Rhoden told researchers that she remembered being:

"one of the first pupils ever to set foot in Launcelot Road School and it was light, airy and wonderful. There were all these beautiful tiles on the wall and I'd never seen anything

---

[56] Ibid, p 48
[57] Ibid p 50

217

like that before. There was a big playground for us to play in as well as small gardens attached to the school"[58]

The advantages of the new estate didn't end there for her:

"What a wonderful childhood we children enjoyed, coming to a new estate with the country on the doorstep, Everyone said the air was like wine. Opposite our road was a field and beyond that an orchard of apples and pears. I remember the hours a friend and I would climb a tree and sit reading our books, munching apples until we felt it was time to go home.

We walked for miles to find different woods and streams and there were loads of ponds around where we'd catch tadpoles and newts."[59]

A lot of kids must have had a lot of fun here and a lot of parents a bit of blessed relief as they let them run off their energy. Which was just as well because the council tried hard to control the behaviour of both adults and children and employed a team of inspectors to make sure you kept to the required standards. Beatrice Kitchen found that:

"When you moved in you had loads of rules to keep. The windows had to be washed every fortnight and the front step cleaned once a week. No mats were to be shaken after ten o'clock. No cats, no dogs, no pets of any kind. You had to keep your children under control at all times.

They didn't give you many warnings and they'd take action against you. They'd send you to the council office if anyone reported your children misbehaving."[60]

The attitude of officials could be deeply patronising. When Phyllis Roden went to the Health Centre because she was

---

[58] Ibid p 68
[59] Ibid p82
[60] Ibid p41

concerned about her child she was bluntly told that she was a bad mother. The doctor:

"was very forthright and would tell you exactly what she thought. I remember her practically insulting me at times and at others praising me to the heavens"[61]

Yet despite all the rules and all the time parents spent trying to bring their children up properly some serious prejudices developed against estate kids. The polite middle-class neighbours living in one set of properties just outside the estate made their views particularly clear. They didn't take at all kindly to a load of estate kids playing anywhere near their own children. Nor did they like the idea of their sons and daughters being chatted up by unsuitable young men and women from the lower orders. The residents of the larger owner-occupied homes at the corner of Valeswood Road and Alexandra Crescent quickly decided that all those well-meaning planners had dumped a problem on them. As soon as 30,000 people got themselves settled into their nice new homes, and their kids happy in their spacious new school their new neighbours sent them a message. They built a 7 foot wall between the new homes and their own. The statement could not have been clearer. We don't want your type here and we would rather have a huge and very inconvenient wall blocking our way than run any risk of social mixing. This astonishing act of deliberate social exclusion must have cast a horrible shadow on those who had worked hard to get themselves out of their crowded and dirty slum and arrive in a wonderful new cottage estate. Only to discover that the wealthy folk just down the road were prepared to go to any lengths to shut them out and to inform them that they still thought they and their kids were scum.

Part of the irony of this notorious physical barrier was that the Downham estate wasn't built for the poorest of the poor. It

---

[61] Ibid p62

was built to enable the respectable working class to live well. The residents who were moved here were those who could be relied on to pay the rent regularly and to look after their homes. Yet they were still viewed with immense suspicion by those who surrounded them. The good people from the right side of the tracks wanted a very clear physical division to keep themselves safe from the riff raff and that wall only got taken down a decade later when fire engines needed to get through the blitz.

I walked down to the old line of division and could find no sign of the blunt exclusion zone that had previously existed. Some of the edges have clearly been rubbed off by time. Few of the homes within the Downham Estate are still in the hands of the council as many residents jumped at the chance to buy them up cheaply and these new owner occupiers have done very well financially out of doing so. Property prices for one of these former council houses are now so high that no young family living off a respectable working-class income could afford to even think about buying one. Indeed they are well beyond the levels of many young middle class Londoners unless they have very significant family support. So there is no longer a huge estate with of mainly working class people all of them renting from the same landlord.

The area has changed significantly. There is, however, still a very clear social divide. On one set of streets outside the old Downham estate you are in solidly affluent semis. On the other you there is still a significant legacy of the old working-class community clinging on despite the modern house prices. The designers of the Downham Estate set out to create a place with a clear identity and succeeded in doing that so firmly that you can still feel the divide on the ground. In the old days, if you lived on the LCC Council Estate then you knew that you belonged there and were often fiercely proud of doing so. If the neighbours didn't like you and put up a wall then so much the worse for them. That identity hasn't just disappeared.

Planners and social reformers leave a legacy – even if it isn't always quite the one that they intended. There is no sign of a wall marking the boundary but there was rarely any moment when I was unsure whether I was inside the old Downham estate or outside it. Anyone who lives here today must be in little doubt that they occupy an area of London that has been consciously planned to be a single entity.

It is fashionable these days to be somewhat critical of well-meaning bureaucrats who plan other people's futures and come up with high minded schemes to help those less fortunate than themselves. I was left with the distinct feeling that in actuality those planners can be proud of what they did here. Creating decent homes for 30,000 people is no small achievement. Doing so with thought and care pays off. The estate is not crumbling into decay. Eighty years after it was built it is still standing proud and attracting fresh buyers. The people who live on the Downham Estate now still have plenty of space surrounding them and are not crammed into endless straight terraces built one against the other without relief. More importantly they have a legacy of community spirit that is almost as tangible as the focus on green spaces that dominates their suburb.

It may be patronising to make decisions on behalf of others but both of the Downham Estates left me feeling that it is, perhaps, a lot better to be patronised by others than simply walled off by them and treated as beneath consideration. Downham in Lancashire has gained a lot by being looked after for a very long time by a single family that knew and understood its community. That family may have unduly dominated that community but it also lived amongst it, shared its concerns and cared about what happened to its residents and to the land and buildings. The evidence of that care can still be seen all around the village. Few of the planers of Downham in London shared the same lifelong connection with one place but they did spend years of their lives working to improve the housing conditions of ordinary working Londoners and put a lot of thought and care into what they provided. They may have had to cut a lot of corners and made a lot of mistakes but they also achieved something of real lasting importance. They provided a very large number of people with homes they could be proud of that they could not possibly have afforded otherwise. And in the process they built a functioning community. Even if the neighbours were ashamed to live alongside them.

****

Downham is a very common name. There are a lot of other places that share it. One of them has a particular importance for me. Downham Market in Norfolk is where my mother was born. For most of its existence it has grown organically for the simple reason that it is situated on one of the very few pieces of genuinely high ground in the depths of the fens. For miles around it the land is flat and featureless. Much of it is so far below sea level that the walls of the drainage ditches are the only thing that rises above the fields. Even the bottom of those ditches is sometimes higher than the farming land that they drain and pumps have to draw up any excessive moisture. In such a wet landscape it made huge sense to gather together on one of the few bits of high land safely above the flood zone and so the town of Downham Market grew up piecemeal across the centuries without any need for a single directing mind to try and plan much of what happened. Then the war came and briefly all that changed. Downham Market went from being a quiet backwater that developed slowly without much conscious planning to being the home for a purpose built military airdrome. A lot of very young men were sent out to their deaths from the fields around Downham Market.

At the start of the Second World War there was a serious shortage of both aircraft and of military airfields in Britain and there were only four in the whole of Norfolk – despite it being an obvious route for enemy bombers to fly over if they wanted to hit cities in the industrial heartland. By the end of the war there were thirty-seven.[62] The nearby flat dry land made for easy building so giant concrete slabs and a collection of rough prefabricated buildings were built from scratch. With incredible rapidity Downham Market got its own airport. Three long runways, a control tower, accommodation, defensive positions and all the other paraphernalia that are needed if you are going to equip bombers to head out into dark skies were created in a few short months. The decision to build there was taken in 1941. Aircraft were taking off on regular raids by 1942. Before long it was home to elite pathfinder crews, many of whom had already completed one tour of 30 flights above cities protected by a barrage of anti-aircraft fire. At certain stages of the war from some airfields the chances of doing that were less than one in 8 so these men had done well to get through their first tour of duty. Their luck or skill in surviving now meant that they were asked to fly in ahead of the other crews and light up the target areas with incendiary devices so that later crews could find their way. This meant that for the air crews it was a seriously dangerous thing to be posted to Downham Market during the second half of the war.

For the locals it was rather different. Especially if you were a pretty young girl. My mother was 14 at the start of the war. Before the airfield was built her choice of admirers was strictly limited. This was a distinctly rural population with a low turnover of population and by your teens you knew every boy that you were ever likely to meet. Then suddenly the airmen arrived and everything was different. In 1942, at the age of 17, my mother found that her options had rapidly expanded to encompass hundreds of young healthy airmen, many of whom had just come back from a life-threatening flight. Something

---

[62] John B Hilling, Strike Hard – A Bomber Airfield at War, (Sutton Publishing, 1997), p2

had to be done to keep up the morale of all these airmen and letting them make the occasional trip to the local pubs or to the village dance was soon on the agenda. A decision of a remote committee of bureaucrats to construct an airfield in this precise location was about to have an explosive effect on the social life of the young women of Downham Market.

From an early age I never had any difficulty in visualising the transformative impact this must have had. My maternal grandfather was a chauffeur who had died of cancer quite young, leaving my grandmother to bring up three children in a small terraced house in Windsor Street on a pathetically small widow's pension. She ran the kind of establishment where the children were expected to scrape out the inside of an egg with a finger if they were lucky enough to get one and where any potato peelings were carefully collected to feed to the chickens to make sure that someone in the family got that egg. The house carried a strong smell of boiled cabbage, had a tiny spiral staircase to take you upstairs to bed, and a front parlour that was kept immaculate but almost never used. Schooling was taken very seriously indeed and, being the youngest, my mother had two extra pairs of eyes watching to make sure that she stuck to her homework if she ever showed any signs of slacking. One of them belonged to a much older sister who was particularly hard working and diligent and the other to a slightly elder brother who was naturally good at everything from sport to academic studies. As a consequence, he held down a job at the railway station – something that was considered an achievement. Until the war started, when he became a Battle of Britain pilot, and my mother took over issuing the tickets and pushing the luggage.

Suddenly the local girl who had lived a very sheltered life was seeing hundreds of young men arriving at her station every day and being asked out repeatedly by them at the weekend dances. My father arrived in early 1944 to work as air crew and found a site so large that a bicycle was the best way to get out to work on the planes. Bitter experience early in the war had determined that it was best to scatter the planes in remote parts of airfields in order to make it harder for one raid to destroy several precious assets. In June 1944, just after the D Day landings, my father spotted my mother at the local cinema and asked her out at the very next dance. Somehow, despite him being posted away to a different location to become a weather observer on planes flying from Ireland far out into the Atlantic they managed to keep the relationship going. As soon as the war was over they joined the post war marriage boom and she found herself living far from Downham Market with two young children.

Once or twice a year we would make the trip over to see her friends and relatives. Traveling in the back of a salesman's car on slow 1950s roads from Urmston Manchester to Downham in Norfolk took a very long time and was desperately tedious for the children in the back. I always associated travelling to Downham Market with a boring journey and an even more boring time being presented for inspection by relatives I scarcely knew. They seemed to be impressed by my ability to grow slightly larger each time I saw them and that was about as interesting as their conversation got. My brother and I moaned every time we were told we were going and showed the usual complete lack of sensitivity to the emotional needs of a parent that most children possess. I decided early on that her home town was a dead-end place that I couldn't wait to get away from.

So when my mother died at the age of 92 after almost 71 years of married life I wanted to go back to Downham Market and explore some of the places that had mattered in her life both to see whether it really was the way that I remembered it and to make some emotional connections with the early part of her life and the place where my parents had met. Finding the station was easy. It was stuck out on the edge of town near the heavily controlled river Ouse and a completely man-made channel designed to drain the fens called the Hundred Foot Drain. The station had a strange Dutch inspired roof that looked like it should have topped a building on an Amsterdam canal and its walls were made of an even stranger mix of building materials including tiny red brown bricks and irregular chunks of local ironstone. Walking through the miniscule ticket hall where my relatives had spent so many hours serving customers I quickly found myself on the platform where they had helped passengers to load and unload their luggage and then waited for the next train so they could do it all again. It was a bleak old place to spend your days. The track went straight as a die across a flat and featureless landscape. There wasn't a lot to look at and even on a gloriously sunny day in mid-summer the view was deeply uninspiring.

I headed off to look for 7 Windsor Street to see if I could get more sense of the past from standing outside my mother's old home. It proved easy enough to locate. A couple of streets away from the station and back from the main road there was a terrace of houses that gave every impression of having changed little since I'd last visited. Not surprisingly the chickens had gone from the garden at the rear but there were still lace curtains protecting the front parlour from prying eyes and my memory hadn't been wrong about quite how small the frontage of the house was. It was the width of that single front room and a thin corridor. I stood outside and visualised the entrance hall leading you into the rear of the home and wondered whether the smell of cabbage was still permeating the kitchen. But I didn't knock and ask to go in and find out. These days people tend to be a little suspicious of strange men arriving at their front door and asking if they can come inside to explore their heritage. Besides I felt I had achieved what I needed to. I had confirmed that my mother's old home was still standing and in reasonable repair. A plaque on the terrace announced that it had been built in 1896 and it looked like it was good for another hundred years or so of providing a reasonable home at a price that a family from the local community could afford.

So I searched next for signs of the old airfield. That took me a short car ride away to the opposite side of town. I drove out to a tiny hamlet called Bexwell and turned off the road into the car park of a small industrial estate. Normally I associate industrial estates with street after street of anonymous factories and warehouses all neatly fitted up and accompanied by bold advertising hoardings announcing which company occupies each plot. This one wasn't remotely like that. It was mostly a collection of rather squalid enterprises that were making use of the cheapest land they could find. Bits of iron girders were left strewn about waiting in case someone might someday have a use for them. There was a burned-out car parked amidst a series of other wrecks that didn't look like anyone was intending to work on restoring or scrapping them any time soon. Bits of concrete blocks had found themselves dumped here for no particular purpose or reason. And dotted around amongst all that decay and neglect there were a series of buildings that seem to have been left over from the war with equal lack of purpose. Out here was where the control tower had been for the airfield and it was in the huts around this part of the site that the men would have been briefed before they were sent out to fly into extreme danger. You could still see a series of long low huts where those young men would have felt sick in the stomach at being told that they had to fly over the Ruhr and get past bank after bank of anti-aircraft barrages and fighter squadrons. Cheap render was peeling off the walls to show equally cheap brickwork beneath. Ivy was climbing onto the corrugated roofs. The memory of those men was not exactly being treasured.

Across the busy A112 there is a very pretty church that some of those airmen would have prayed in either to remember their friends who had not returned or to try and secure a little extra hope that some God was looking out for their survival.

227

Next to it I found a well maintained and respectful memorial to two of the men from this airfield who had won the Victoria Cross for acts of extreme bravery. The inscriptions describing what these young people had done brought home some of the horror of the experience. Bleeding on the floor of a shot up airplane whilst you try and talk your surviving crewmate through the best way to land a plane on a runway in Algeria without the benefit of any prior experience is a long slow and painful way for a young pilot to use up the last hours of his life. The strain of doing that killed one of the VC winners but it kept his friends alive. That kind of self-sacrifice is well worthy of being remembered.

A mile or so away on the other side of the airfield there is a neighbouring little hamlet with an equally pretty church at a place called Wimbotsham. From near here I crossed another busy A road and walked on a track through a long field of wheat towards the very centre of the former airfield. About half a mile up the track I reached a section of the old runway. Consulting the maps in my books on the history of the airfield suggested that this must have been runway B[63]. What looked like a fifty foot wide strip of concrete had been left intact amongst the wheat field and was running at right angles from the track I had walked up. It headed straight towards Downham Market. Much of the runway had crumbled under the impact of 70 years of weathering but in other sections you could still see a thin layer of bitumen that had been hastily sprayed over concrete as the runway was rushed to be completed. On a miserable night in 1944 one of the bombers speeding down one of the three runways carrying a full load of bombs failed to get into the air quickly enough. It went straight into a hut occupied by troops on the ground and exploded. My father remembers that no one was told how many people had died and that when he was asked whether he would be prepared to volunteer to clean up the dead body

---

[63] Ibid, p7

parts he recognised that it was beyond his ability to cope with the horrors of such an experience and he declined the opportunity. I couldn't say I blamed him.

As I was contemplating their fate and trying to work out whether this was the runway where they had died I saw another person out walking the runway along the runway. As he approached he asked me whether I was from the building firm. When I said that I didn't understand the question and was just out here exploring the airfield he explained why he assumed someone with maps and taking notes was from a housing developer. Apparently, there are plans to build over the field where the runway lies and it is just a matter of time before the site is transformed. I found myself in two minds about the change. It is not particularly respectful of the memory of those who sacrificed young lives to put up a housing estate across the last piece of land they were on before they set off to their deaths. On the other hand, it is also not particularly respectful to leave the buildings they were briefed in to crumble into the ground in the middle of the run down remnants of an industrial estate that has clearly failed to attract much industry. I also felt in two minds about the loss of this particular bit of green land to the bulldozers. It is sad to see any piece of agricultural land lost to a housing estate but it was difficult to see the environmental benefits of preserving a giant monocultured wheat field. I had walked past 800 yards or so of the same crop growing on every inch of ground. Ahead of me there was another 800 yards of the same thing. The only way of growing one crop over this length of countryside is to spray enough pesticides on it to keep any insect life away and to pour enough nitrates onto the soil to ensure that it doesn't become infertile. A housing estate with a variety of plants and a few ponds dotted around in the new gardens was almost certainly going to generate more variety of wildlife than this particular bit of countryside. I was left hoping that local farmers might one day get the help and support they need to make it affordable to grow crops in less sterile and alienating way than these great blocks of wheat fields. I was also left hoping that whoever does plonk a new housing estate on this site finds some way of doing so whilst paying respect to its heritage. Above all I was left feeling that it would be wonderful if someone could find the money and the imagination to rescue the last few remaining buildings dotted around amongst the detritus of the failed industrial estate and provide future generations with better opportunities to appreciate what had happened here.

At the moment It is all too easy to walk across this environment and feel as if the events of the Second World War had never happened here. The airmen and their runways arrived when they were needed and departed when they weren't. There are a few stretches of crumbling concrete left and many of the huts that were hastily thrown up are slowly sinking back into the ground but the town of Downham Market had been left largely untouched. There are memories of the sudden influx of airmen amongst a few very elderly people and tales of them have been passed down to living relatives. But the town does not appear to have been changed in any significant way in its course of evolution. In the other two Downhams the plans of a very few important and powerful individuals changed the course of the history of the locality for ever. In Downham Lancashire the result was a landscape dominated by the power of one family. In Downham London the result was a very particular kind of housing and a certain proud defiance in being from the Estate. But in Downham Market in Norfolk the impact of the military planners was purely temporary. Sometimes the decisions made by influential people are of huge importance and can transform the lives of generations. At other times it is remarkable how little impact they leave behind. Except, of course, for those like myself who know that their own existence is entirely the product of the passing momentary decision making of some remote civil servant who was solely interested in trying to please superiors and win a war.

Postscript

The selection of places I have chosen to describe in this book is pretty arbitrary. There are plenty of other locations that share a name and several of the places I described have other partners in the UK that I was aware of but chose not to describe. I tried to pick environments where I knew something already about one of the partners and much less at first about the other. I also tried to choose places which any outsider would tend to believe had either absolutely nothing in common or were fundamentally very similar. Neither proved to be the case in practice.

Anyone who has lived in or around the places I have visited in writing this may well have found plenty to disagree with. It is impossible to write about people's home territory without saying things that seem unfair or just plain wrong to those with local knowledge. In my defence it is worth saying that what I set out to do was not to provide a series of dry factual descriptions of the history and current circumstances of these places. All of them do have fascinating local histories and most of them already have very good local historians whose books I found well worth reading. I was trying to do something very different. I wanted to give a feel for what it is like for an outsider to explore these areas and I wanted to tell the stories that most interested me as I did so. I tried to look into the less familiar aspects of these places and to uncover things that other people might not look into. Put simply I set out to have fun exploring and to try and communicate some of that enjoyment both in what I saw and what I read. I thought that approach might enable me to discover some surprises both for myself and for others.

So my apologies to any readers who felt that the most important things about their locality weren't even mentioned or that I was unfairly rude about somewhere that they care about. I was trying to help people to look at a locality in a different way. For example, I never for one minute thought

231

that on the strength of a bit of reading and a short visit I could reveal the essence of Newcastle Upon Tyne to the locals. I did think I might be able to use my knowledge of history to explore some of the layers within the city that few locals get round to visiting very often. But what you discover on a visit isn't always what you expect. I ended up finding out a lot more about the different ways two of our most important urban areas had dealt with decades of industrial decline. In doing so I was probably far too generous to the planners of Newcastle Upon Tyne and far too pessimistic about the efforts to generate Newcastle Under Lyme. My only excuse is that on the days when I chose to visit that was how it genuinely looked to an outsider.

In much the same way as I stumbled across places when I walked through them I also found that taking a trip through the history of these areas also didn't reveal quite what I expected. When I read about the two Bradfords I thought I would uncover a tale of two very different histories - instead I was constantly surprised by how much history they had in common. Both had built up successful textile industries. Both had experienced serious pollution and periods of industrial decline. Yet the difference between them was staggeringly stark. One has become very wealthy. The other has not. And desperately few people who live in the two locations know anything much about the way people in the other live their lives.

We live in a country of extreme contrasts and yet share certain histories. Despite all the hours of television that we have available for us those contrasts and commonalities are rarely seen. The poorest areas of our nation only seem to appear on television if someone wants to show up their citizens as being objects of curiosity. They are either the worthy poor struggling against heroic odds or much more commonly portrayed as feckless wasters. Those who live in wealthier areas or in the suburbs can be almost equally well hidden. It was beyond my ability to properly uncover both sets of lives and address any Imbalance. How could anyone even begln to explore something that in reality is so diverse and complex?

What I have tried to do instead is to explore those differing towns and landscapes with an open mind. In doing so I discovered for myself just how much more interesting and varied those places are than any stereotype. I hope you have been able to share some of the enjoyment of those discoveries as you read this book.

When we are children there is a tendency to assume that the places where we live have always been there and we take them for granted. Even as we age it is surprisingly difficult to visualise a town or a landscape as something that has been handed down to us as the result of conscious decisions made by people in the past. Undertaking the research and the journeys for this book has brought home to me just how strongly I have shared that prejudice. It isn't just the towns that I have visited that have been shaped and transformed by history and by the decisions on individuals. It is also the countryside that surrounds those towns. Little of the British countryside has been left intact and untouched. Even in the wildest of places like the uplands of the two river Dees you quickly find evidence of human intervention and realise that you are walking a landscape that has been changed and re-changed. If that is true of our wilder uplands then it is even more true of our cities and our towns. Places that we think of today as being beautiful untouched country towns like Bradford on Avon turn out under close inspection to have been hotbeds of industry. Today's delightful trout stream turns out to have once been ruined by the filthy stench of the run off from dye works.

I think that means there can be only one clear message from this book. The decisions that we make about our communities and our places matter. Make the right decisions and our generation will leave a legacy that the next generation will be proud of. Make the wrong ones and their judgements of us might be even harsher than even the most critical ones that we tend to make of our predecessors.

Printed in Poland
by Amazon Fulfillment
Poland Sp. z o.o., Wrocław